JESUS'
FAMILY
VALUES

For I have come to set a man against his father,
and a daughter against her mother,
and a daughter-in-law against her mother-in-law;
and one's foes will be members of one's own household.

Whoever loves father or mother more than me is not worthy of me; and whoever loves son or daughter more than me is not worthy of me. . . .

—MATTHEW 10:35–37

JESUS' FAMILY VALUES

DEIRDRE GOOD

CHURCH PUBLISHING
an imprint of
Church Publishing Incorporated, New York

Library of Congress Cataloging-in-Publication Data

Good, Deirdre Joy.
    Jesus' family values / Deirdre Good.
       p.   cm.
    Includes bibliographical references.
    ISBN-13: 978-1-59627-027-5
    ISBN-10: 1-59627-027-6
    1. Family – Biblical teaching. 2. Family – Religious aspects –
Christianity.   I. Title.
    BS2545.F33G66 2006
    261.8'3585 – dc22

                                    2006024427

Church Publishing Incorporated
445 Fifth Avenue
New York, NY 10016
www.churchpublishing.org

5 4 3 2 1

Alexander the Great shaped much about the world of Jesus, its values and families. After Darius's defeat by Alexander, Darius's mother, Sisygambis, went to kneel in supplication before Alexander. When she mistakenly knelt in front of the taller figure of Hephaestion, historians record that Alexander forgave her, saying, "Don't worry, Mother, he too is Alexander." Veronese depicts this scene in his painting *The Family of Darius before Alexander.* Alexander stands with outstretched arms, including in his gesture both Sisygambis with her children and Hephaestion. By calling Sisygambis "Mother" and by identifying Hephaestion with himself, Alexander brings the family of his vanquished enemy, along with his closet comrade, into his own family. Magnanimity creates families both then and now.

This book is dedicated to my family.

CONTENTS

ACKNOWLEDGMENTS

WITHOUT several people this book would never have come into being. Thanks to an invitation from Rabbi Leonard Schoolman, the book originated as a course on Jesus and Family Values taught in the Center for Religious Inquiry at St. Bartholomew's Church, in New York City. I would like to acknowledge Lenny's commitment and the commitment of Billy Tully, the rector of St. Bartholomew's, to excellent adult educational offerings.

As for the book itself, Julian Sheffield is its co-creator. Thanks also go to Tim Burger, Diane Apostolos-Cappadona, Peter Gomes, Bishops Cathy Roskam and Krister Stendahl, Alan Segal, Alistair Steward-Sykes, and Sandy Squire.

Chapter One

THE BIBLE AND FAMILY VALUES

WHEN I WAS ABOUT THIRTEEN, I wrote an essay for homework on the importance of wood in modern life. Having identified only two items, namely, telegraph poles and wooden shafts in mines to support tunnel construction, I asked my mother's opinion. "What's the most important thing wood is used for today?" I asked her. "A bed," she said. I was sufficiently taken aback to remember the story to this day. However, her answer points not just to the need for rest (at that time my father, an ordained priest, was working in a teacher training college, and she had her own job as a physiotherapist, in addition to household responsibilities that included two teenagers), but to the importance of structures of support for her life and that of her family. She herself, of course, was the primary "structure of support" for her husband and children, and while she considered a bed to be the most important use of wood, no mere thing would be the most important support structure in her life.

To this day my parents' primary support structures include each other, daily prayer time together, the routine of daily work despite "retirement," meals, recreation, and affection shared, as well as work and recreation taken apart from each other. The needs and difficulties and interests attendant upon a large network of extended family and parish relationships provide a different kind

of support for my parents, who have both a vocation and passion for ministry. Their baptismal vows, marriage vows, and his
ordination vows are crucial structures of support for them and
have remained constant through radically different settings — rural East Africa where two children were born and raised; urban
England with two adolescents growing up; tropical Fiji, far distant from any relatives; urban England again, but this time with
responsibility for an aging parent.

This core family of two adults and two children looks very
much like the archetypal conservative Christian family promoted
by groups like James Dobson's Focus on the Family. The sources
of support for this family — the God of Jesus Christ, Holy Scripture, purpose-driven lives — seem very similar, if not identical,
to the sources of support for mine. But move one degree out
of my core family into the extended family, and every possible
variation that can be found in modern Western society exists — except perhaps polygamy, although I couldn't absolutely guarantee
that! There are divorces, remarriages, step-relatives, partnerships
(heterosexual and homosexual) without benefit of marriage, ex-
spouses and ex-spouses' children. There are people in my extended
family for whom there are no English terms to describe the nature
and degree of relationship.

Further, there are lots of people in my extended family, related to me by no more than one degree of separation, for whom
the sources of support my parents' generation consider indispensable — the God of Jesus Christ, Holy Scripture — are peripheral
if not meaningless. And there are still more members who find
their sources of support in scriptural Christianity but understand
family as far larger than those related by blood or indissoluble
marriage. But what characterizes my extended family members
as family is an extraordinary degree of permanence within flux
and change, brought about by the family's own response to itself.
Every divorce, every relationship without benefit of marriage has
caused my parents deep distress and consternation; but every ex-
spouse, new spouse, unmarried partner remains in their thoughts,

love, prayers, and, perhaps more tellingly, on the guest list of their fiftieth wedding anniversary.

But would all religious groups understand that my family reflects legitimate "family values"? Yes, according to a 2005 *Valuing Families* resource on the Web site of the National Council of Churches (USA). The package "is designed to inspire Christian families to honor and prayerfully support families of all shapes and sizes" and connect them with discussions and activities to help them identify and appreciate the many characteristics that shape families today. Focus on the Family, on the other hand, proscribes sex outside of marriage for believers (whether homosexual or heterosexual). While the group understands scripture to condemn homosexuality and premarital heterosexuality, it mandates acceptance of those violating these ordinances, as we can see in the example of Jesus' compassion for the women taken in adultery. Similarly, *FamilyLife.com* explains that conservative evangelicals understand God to release people from the lifelong covenant of marriage in only two circumstances: consistent and unrepentant immorality (based on a reading of Matt. 19:7–9) and when an unbelieving spouse deserts a believer (based on a reading of 1 Cor. 7:15–17).

What exactly are family values and where do they come from? If you Google "family values" you might find, "Looking for Family Values? Find exactly what you want today. *www.ebay.com.*" Values become whatever you want them to be on eBay. But if you tried a similar search on texts that existed in Jesus' time, you would be in trouble immediately. There is no word in Greek or Hebrew that exactly corresponds to the modern word "family"; the closest Greek word, *oikia,* or *oikos,* means variously household or house, like *bet* in Hebrew, which similarly means house and can be used for household in the sense of family lineage. Two other Hebrew words used for related groups of people are *toldot* and *mishpachah,* generations and clan or tribe. Similarly with the word "values" — any Greek or Hebrew word that might be translated "value" refers specifically to monetary or market worth. Of course, our word "family" comes from the Latin word *familia,* but for the Romans, the meaning and the reality were far more similar to the Greek *oikia* and the Hebrew *bet* than to our modern "family," as we shall see.

So if we can't find "family values" anywhere in the Bible, or in the linguistic world of Jesus, when and where does the phrase begin to appear? What constitutes family values and who decides? What can we find in the teachings of Jesus or other Christian scripture that speaks to family values today? What would "family" have looked like in the world and time of Jesus? Is there any scriptural warrant for elevating "family values" to a primary position in Christian belief systems today? What would a scripture-defined "family" look like today, and what would its "values" be? These are the questions that we will explore.

Where Do Family Values Come From?

Most Americans assume the exclusively domestic function and private character of our houses, and we identify the home as a place of refuge from daily work. The pinnacle of the American Dream is home ownership, and the preferred home is the one-family house. But these are modern ideas going back only to the Victorian period. When we consider the home as a place for the raising of children, we must remember that childhood as we know it, an extended time of sheltered nurturing, was practically invented by the Victorians, and reserved to wealthy families. Suburbia as a bedroom community for the city originated in the Victorian period with the advent of rapid public transit. When people use the term "traditional family," what is meant may look a lot more like a Victorian family than a family in the time of Jesus.

For example, Victorian religious art ordinarily depicts the Holy Family as a calm, detached, affluent nuclear family, typified by James Collinson's *The Holy Family.* Here a young, healthily padded woman sits on an invisible seat in front of the corner of a red brick building set in a garden with hollyhocks. Her carefully draped dress and cloak are immaculate, as is her person. Under a simple nimbus, a pure white veil with no visible means of anchoring partially covers her hair. The child stands in perfect composure on her knee, reaching out to a dove resting on Joseph's hand. Joseph, also with nimbus, wears a long clean garment under a cloak whose careful folds mark a citizen of leisure; his hair and beard have been professionally groomed. Each character wears an expression of serene gravity. Behind the tableau a cypress frames a calm meandering river under a blue sky with a few tentative clouds.

A significant departure from this pattern is John Everett Millais' *Christ in the House of His Parents,* also known as *The Carpenter's Shop.* The controversy surrounding this work suggests the extent to which Victorians considered the Holy Family to be elevated above and apart from the experience of ordinary working-class family life. Millais clearly understood that Joseph's carpentry shop was located in the house, a confusion of contexts abhorrent to the emerging Victorian ideal that particular places be reserved for particular functions, and that the home be protected from the incursions of work. For a twenty-first-century viewer, however, the painting is a perfectly respectable representation of an extended family at work in some ancient period. In the center a mother kneels comforting a child perhaps ten years old, clad in a white shift, who has hurt his hand. All of the figures in the painting lean toward the wounded boy in concern; the younger apprentice, perhaps John the Baptist since his breeches are made of some wild animal's fur, carries a bowl of water for cleansing the wound. The shop is clean, littered only with the expected wood shavings; lumber is stacked and tools hung tidily in the background; a dove hunching on a ladder behind the table watches the child with a worried look. The door of the shop reveals a pastoral landscape with green fields under a blue sky beyond; from a pen of clean farm animals close to the house, even the rams and sheep focus upon the child with concern. The Victorian outcry against the painting may demonstrate the extent to which working-class life was considered incompatible with the upbringing of children and the maintenance of a proper home. So deeply was the understanding of respectable family divorced from the reality of working-class life that Millais is recorded as having hoped that Queen Victoria's private viewing of the painting had not been too "corrupting."

The term "family values" was popularized in the Republican presidential campaign of 1992 after Dan Quayle attributed the then recent Rodney King riots in Los Angeles to a "breakdown of family structure, personal responsibility and social order," and then cited as "mocking fatherhood" the TV sitcom *Murphy Brown,* in which Brown chooses to bear and raise a child by herself, rather than to abort. While a number of the components of the current "family values" debate have been in public and political contention for decades, the current debate about "family values" as a package dates to 1992.

In 1980 a White House "Conference on Families" took place, and in 1983 the Family Research Council associated with James Dobson was incorporated. The Family Research Council (FRC) extols the virtue and value of the two-parent, marriage-based family as the foundation of society. According to its Web site, the FRC holds that marriage can only be the life-long union of one man and one woman, and believes that sexual relations should occur only within lawful marriage.

In scholarly circles, it was also in the 1980s that several publications appeared on family, house, and house church in the period of Christian origins. By the mid-eighties a consensus existed: households were at the center of the mission of the early Christian movement. The house church was vital for local churches or assemblies, serving as a focal point for prayer, Eucharist, and instruction. It was a base for outreach, and as a community it was a place to experience and exercise fellowship or love of brothers (and sisters). Early believers of the Christ cult existed in a wider social world. Architectural evidence from Dura-Europos indicates that Jews, followers of the Roman cult of Mithras, and

Christians all adapted private homes for worship purposes. As far as the New Testament is concerned, evidence from Luke and Matthew indicates that from 50 to 150 CE early believers met in the private homes of wealthy members of the group. Since the gatherings included a common meal, they probably took place in a dining room or living quarters. Nothing distinguishes the buildings that hosted such assemblies from domestic houses. Subsequently, larger houses were probably altered and used in part or perhaps primarily for worship. At the same time, believers probably continued to meet in houses. In the mid-second century, a gradual expansion to larger buildings and halls is evident.

Once the centrality of the *oikos* as the basic social, legal, and economic unit within Hellenistic and Roman society and the importance of the *oikos* as a place of individual and public identity was understood, studies on networks of the *oikos* and the family took on a new importance. Moreover the wider political North American context in which scholarship has occurred since the 1980s (and probably before) gives such academic undertakings a particular relevance.

A major distinction between traditional and progressive scholarship concerns the application of biblical material: traditional scholarship views the Bible prescriptively while progressive scholarship views biblical material primarily descriptively and secondarily considers its current application. Traditional scholarship regards biblical teaching on marriage and family as a blueprint for the modern home. There is no gap between the text and my life. Progressive scholarship prefers to "mind the gap" and to describe as fully as possible historical contexts in which meaning is disclosed as the first step toward understanding biblical statements on marriage and family. For example, material from Hebrew scriptures has an entirely different social, economic, and historical context from material in the New Testament. Observing this historical context respects the historical circumstances in which divine disclosure took place. Paying attention to historical contexts goes some way toward preventing an interpreter from projecting his or her own mental landscape onto the text.

Recent traditional writing (e.g., Andreas Köestenberger, *God, Marriage, and Family*) understands marriage and the family to be the primary divinely instituted order for the human race. These institutions are to be characterized by monogamy, fidelity, heterosexuality, fertility, complementarity, and permanence. (Note the prescriptive language: these institutions *are to be* characterized . . .). The New Testament, Köestenberger continues, defines marital roles in terms of respect and love as well as submission and authority. While there is "neither male nor female" as far as salvation in Christ is concerned (Gal. 3:28), there remains a pattern in which the wife is to emulate the church's submission to Christ and the husband is to imitate Christ's love for the church (Eph. 5:21–33). The married couple witnesses to surrounding culture and ought to understand itself within the larger framework of God's end-time purposes in Christ. Again, note the prescriptive language: "the wife *is to emulate*," "the husband *is to imitate*," "the married couple . . . *ought to understand*." How do we know marriage and family is the primary divinely instituted order of the human race? By what means is marriage and the family selected over any other divinely instituted human institution? Such a judgment indicates that there are some covert presuppositions operating to privilege marriage and family over anything else. As for "neither male nor female" in Galatians 3:28, the text is misquoted. The original text actually reads, "there is no male *and* female," alluding specifically to the text of Genesis 1:27, the creation of humanity as "male and female"; what baptism into Christ does is to transcend the original complementarity, not to perpetuate the polarity. In other words, in Pauline thought, baptism creates an identity exclusive of gender, whether that means by unifying the male and female, or by creating an entirely gender-free category. Galatians dispenses with gender categories, Ephesians emphasizes them; by subordinating Galatians to Ephesians, Köestenberger overrides Paul's mandate for gender-free baptismal life in Christ, and reinscribes sexual differences as operative. This is an example of how certain texts are privileged in support of a modern traditional understanding of marriage; most scholars would agree that Ephesians was not written by Paul, and therefore should not be elevated over Galatians, which everyone agrees was written by Paul.

Surely marriage today is not the same thing as marriage in Eden or in ancient Israel, or in the time of Jesus. It is too obvious to say that there is no one single understanding of marriage in the Bible and that collapsing teaching on marriage and family into one single model reduces diversity to the point of distortion. Moreover, Jesus wasn't married, and Paul seems to commend singleness or sexual asceticism over marriage. What do Jesus' singleness and Paul's commendations imply for the human condition? If barrenness is generally viewed as divine disfavor, is Jesus the exception that proves the rule? What does this say about Paul?

There is no one understanding of social roles of parents, either in the Old or New Testaments. Why should a passage from 1 Timothy 2:15 or Titus 2:4–5 be selected to prescribe women's God-given calling as wives and homemakers? What about New Testament descriptions of women's prophetic roles as wives and mothers, as is the case with Jesus' mother? Finally, in Köstenberger's whole book, there seems to be no discussion of slavery, whether in ancient Israel or in the Hellenistic or Roman worlds. This omission is a problem. Slavery was normative in the world of Jesus' time. Even poor households employed slaves. Not to know something about the role of slaves in a household or family setting is to have a partial, not to say distorted, view of New Testament texts.

Carolyn Osiek and Margaret MacDonald's *A Woman's Place: House Churches in Earliest Christianity* points out that modern literary and rhetorical analysis of ancient male-authored texts has increased our awareness that ancient descriptions of men and women promote authorial agendas rather than describe real people. Nevertheless, these scholars claim to discover a more

expanded role than the dutiful wife in Ephesians, and to identify women as patrons, teachers, and dinner hosts with influence
in households and house church communities. Women could
be married, divorced, widowed, or martyred. *A Woman's Place*
interprets archaeological material from catacombs as showing
women taking leadership roles in family funerary banquets. Ancient sources assuming domestic slavery, the authors suggest,
indicate that the topic of whether to hire a wet nurse or nurse
the baby oneself was of great interest. If one hires a wet nurse,
what kind of nurse has the best influence on the life of the young
child? Understanding such questions to reflect concerns of mothers (or fathers) at the time of Christian origins "minds the gap"
by indicating distance between ancient and modern concerns.

Traditional family values proponents claim that biblical authority as they construe it overrides all other authorities and warrants
imposition on all Americans. Second, they hold that the only
scripturally warranted family consists of a male and a female in
monogamous lifelong marriage and their children, and only such
constellations should be accorded the legal protections and privileges enjoyed by families. Third, they usually locate scriptural
authority in the specific words of an English translation (such as
the King James Version) read out of context and with minimal
reference to the historical context or the linguistic world of the
source. Such a reading of scripture, by definition, assumes permanence of meaning and a fixed context which admits of little
interpretation. By this means order and unity are imposed upon
scripture, and when that is not possible, certain texts — such as
those favoring the submission of women — are privileged while
others, equally authoritative, are suppressed.

Opinions about the authority of scripture vary among the main
divisions of Christianity: Orthodox, Catholic, and Protestant do
not agree; books from the Second Temple period of Judaism written in Greek, called the Apocrypha, are included in Catholic and
Orthodox Bibles but are generally absent from Protestant. Within
mainstream denominations that use a Sunday lectionary, some

biblical texts are privileged over others. In evangelical churches, it is the individual pastor or a worship committee who selects the texts to be read, preached, or studied, raising the level of authority of those texts. Scripture, which as we have seen actually means *some scriptures,* is considered the ultimate authority in many Protestant and evangelical churches, while tradition, doctrine, church hierarchy, or reason may have equal weight in Catholic, Orthodox, and some Protestant churches. And since scripture cannot pick and choose its own advocates, even where *sola scriptura* rules in theory, the authority of scripture itself is moderated by the fact that it must be interpreted and mediated through human language and translation. Even if we all spoke fluently the *Koine* Greek in which the New Testament was written, we would be interpreting the scripture through our own time and our own understanding of meaning.

If we accept that scripture is in some way authoritative, then we must give it the respectful, critical, and intelligent attention due to a text that is both a document from a definite historical period as well as, we believe, a living channel for understanding God's direction and purpose for us. This means we must be willing to acknowledge the limitations placed by time and place on a historical document and at the same time discover its implications for the time and place in which we live today. So to see if there is any relationship between the Jesus of scripture and our current national obsession with "family values," we must begin with the similarities and differences between our modern families and the households of antiquity, reading scripture closely to see what guidelines lie therein and how we may responsibly apply them.

From Household to Home

Today, we recognize the household's importance for preindustrial societies: it gave individuals identity and, ideally, security within a domestic structure or home, and it provided access to networks in the world outside. The *oikos* (house, household) and the *polis* (city) support and undergird each other; the household, as Cicero says, is the fundamental unit of the state (*On Duties* 53–5). The ability for a man to regulate his own household is prerequisite to his responsible functioning in the public forum, according to Plutarch (*Advice to Bride and Groom,* 43); similarly 1 Timothy requires that an overseer in the church be someone who manages his own household well. The citizens in the earliest Greek cities were those who could trace their lineage back to the founding households of the city, while the organization of the city itself was undertaken to provide common services for its households: protection, sanitation, a marketplace, a legal system, and sites for public worship. Households are also expected to provide the personnel and the funding for the functioning of the city. Of course, domestic and public buildings in Jesus' time varied in size, shape, and organization from region to region, but in general a significant part of the ancient domicile was a place where the city and the household interacted, a public space within the home.

Archaeological evidence helps us to analyze actual structures so that we can reconstruct buildings and identify their functions and component parts in different locations. Literary texts, however, have been produced by the literate, and as such are shaped by the social location, point of view, and agendas of their writers. When we use these texts for evidence about the past, we have to be able to discern whether they are describing actual conditions, or prescribing the way things ought to be or might have been, in the mind of the writer. This is not always easy. Most of the written historical evidence we have for household and family life falls into this category, including the New Testament and the writings of authors like Cicero and Plutarch. Nonliterary texts — laundry lists, shopping lists, inventories of storehouses, sales records, brief letters home from common soldiers and merchants — are less subject to the bias of the authors, and as such are incredibly useful as evidence even if what they are witness *to* is not always self-evident. Consider the problems anyone else might have interpreting the most recent list you wrote on the back of an envelope; the classic sci-fi novel *A Canticle for Leibowitz* is based on this difficulty.

Architecture as evidence has its own integrity and provides a separate witness to household and civil life that avoids some of the limitations and problems of literary texts, but ancient architectural components are frequently fragmentary, rarely labeled, and may have been removed from the original site. The more durable domestic structures are by necessity the more expensive, and therefore more likely to attest to the lives of the privileged. Responsible archaeologists today treat material evidence with the same attention to detail as we find in crime scene investigations, and with many of the same operating principles: the site of the find provides vital clues and must be studied and protected, and the interpretation must not be prejudiced by reading our own cultural biases back into the evidence.

Language about Families and Households

If we want to learn how Jesus would assess the various configurations and promotions of family and family values today, we must also examine the specific language used in the Bible. That is why this section involves some close attention to word study. Although we will try to find connections and similarities between the ancient conceptions and our own, we also have to recognize the profound differences, the otherness of the world in which Jesus lived.

As I said earlier, all reading of scripture requires translation, even for those who are trained in the original ancient language. Translators choose along a whole spectrum of possible English words to render the connotations of the underlying Greek, Hebrew, and Aramaic texts. There is rarely an exact one-to-one equivalence in vocabulary, and the use of syntax in the original language may influence meaning in a way that is hard to render in another. In some translations the choice of the English word may be influenced by doctrinal beliefs, but far more often the shape of a translation is determined by a particular theory — either the *formal equivalence* model or the *dynamic equivalence* model. Translators who adopt the former try to render the original into English in a way that preserves as much as possible the philological root meaning and the syntactic patterns of the original; the resulting text thereby retains its sense of foreign-ness. Translations made using the dynamic equivalence model have a different goal: they try to render the source text into language that will be as familiar to us as the original language was to the original audience. This means that if an idiomatic expression is used in the Greek, the translator will provide a similar, more colloquial English translation rather than trying to reproduce the literal, formal meaning.

Awareness of these options in translation helps us when we look at specific words that signal discussions about families or households in the Bible. If a translator wants to emphasize the similarities between then and now, how will the translation look by comparison with the translation that makes the source context seem far away from us? Just as archaeologists need to examine artifacts in their physical context, it is only by looking at the context of specific words that we can get a sense of how these words work to build an understanding of the world in which Jesus lived. Many of these citations appear in passages that are read and preached on in church, so the focus is usually on spiritual or ethical content; here, we are bringing into the foreground details that normally serve as background, so that we can build a picture of the typical environment for the kind of family Jesus would have known.

In the *Koine* or common Greek of the New Testament period, two words, *oikos* and *oikia,* provided an umbrella for discussion of all things pertaining to the household and the family. Each of these root words has certain connotations reserved to it, while there is also some overlap, but scholars have not yet been able to isolate the precise shades of meaning that dictate the particular choice of one word over the other. We know that English has very specific words that describe dwelling places — hovel, shanty, mobile home, apartment, farmhouse, condo — and convey different implications for family life; but family members go "home" to all of them. Archaeology tells us that a similar degree of variation in styles of domicile existed in antiquity, but we cannot be certain exactly how the usage of *oikos* and *oikia* relates to these differences. In general, *oikos* has architectural connotations, while *oikia* connotes sociology, that is, composition of a household.

The primary definition for the word *oikos* is house, whether a built house or any dwelling place, with subsets of house appearing also, such as room or chamber, and other places for congregating, such as meetinghouse, hall, treasury, or the temple; even cage and beehive are included. A secondary definition is household goods, or substance; in an earlier period of the Greek language, it was used in legal writing for estate, property left at death, or inheritance. Third, *oikos* can denote a royal family dynasty, as in Luke's description of Joseph as of "the *oikos* and lineage of David." Additionally, Acts 18:8 has a sociological connotation: "And Crispus, the official of the synagogue, became a believer in the Lord, together with his whole *oikos*." Here the word would be rendered "household," deriving from the third usage, and overlapping with the sociological connotations of the related word *oikia*.

The primary definition of *oikia* is architectural: a building, house, or dwelling. *Oikia* is used more frequently than *oikos* and compares to *oikos* as a set of apartments or rooms compares to house. In the earlier legal writing referred to above, *oikia* would refer exclusively to the dwelling place included in the property. When it refers to apartments, it would be one's own apartments, not lodgings rented to others. A second definition for *oikia* is sociological: a household or domestic establishment and, more specifically, the inmates of the house. A second sociological usage overlaps with a usage for *oikos*, the family from which one is descended, without the royal connotations of *oikos*.

Since the architectural definition is primary for both *oikos* and *oikia*, physical descriptions of buildings, rooms, and related edifices are the first category for our examination of the language in the New Testament. For example, Mark's Gospel says, "While Jesus was at Bethany in the *house* of Simon the leper, as he reclined at table, a woman came with an alabaster jar of very costly ointment of nard, and she broke open the jar and poured ointment on his head" (Mark 14:3). The people who are present begin to complain about the waste of expensive luxury, but if we imagine ourselves as guests at the home of an associate, we can realize what is truly astonishing: the woman simply arrives without anyone noticing or finding it strange. One could conjecture that her obvious affluence warrants her entry, but what is clear is that such a dinner, in such a place, is a far more public event than we would expect it to be. Jesus and Simon the leper are not secluded in a private room: they are completely accessible while they are having dinner.

The sociological use of the word *oikia,* household, occurs in Mark 13:34–35: "It's like a man going on a journey: he leaves his *house* and puts his slaves in charge, each with his work, and commands the doorkeeper to be on the watch. Therefore, watch — for you do not know when the master of the *house* will come. . . . " At first read *oikia* seems to connote simply a dwelling, but upon further consideration it becomes clear that Mark refers to the entire household remaining awake. Some translations prefer to render the word *oikia* in 13:34 as "home" and translate: "when he leaves home" (RSV, NRSV, NJB, TEV). This is a significant shift; to modern readers it sounds like a first-century traveler leaving a secluded, private area. Is this translation warranted or even correct? It seems to me the most we can say about this "master of the house" is that he owns several slaves to whom he can entrust the household, or estate, when he goes away. If by "home" we mean the modern notion of a private refuge inhabited only by family members and not servants, then it is probably misleading to translate "home" here.

To simplify, we can agree that in the Greek translation of Hebrew scriptures (the Septuagint, or LXX) or the New Testament and contemporary Greek literature, the Greek word *oikos* connotes "building" or "structure," and *oikia* connotes "household." The meaning of *oikos* can also overlap with *oikia* to imply household, namely, those living under the same roof. In 1 Corinthians 1:16, Paul remembers that he baptized the household (*oikos*) of Stephanas. In this aspect, it belongs to the semantic domain of words describing persons related by blood, namely, race, ethnic group or nation (*genos, sarx*), tribe, clan, or nation (*phule*), relatives and kinsfolk (*genea, suggeneia*), and one's own people (*hoi idioi*).

The merging of *oikos/oikia* to connote house or household is interesting. Modern translations make scarcely any distinctions. Of the Gospel writers, only Luke seems to differentiate at all between the two terms: with some exceptions, Luke uses *oikos* in the sense of an edifice, and *oikia* in the sense of household. Scholarship recognizes in the author of Luke-Acts a careful writer who would know and observe nuances of vocabulary; this writer was deliberate in the choice to use *oikos* or *oikia*, even if the organizing principles of those choices remain opaque to us. Luke 10:5 demonstrates both Luke's recognition of distinctions and our uncertainty about what those distinctions might be: Jesus enjoins itinerant disciples, "Whatever *oikia* (household, dwelling) you enter, first say 'Peace to this *oikos* [a particular house, or building, designated by the demonstrative *this*].'" From the nouns *oikos* and *oikia*, moreover, derive a number of verbs indicating living, dwelling, or inhabiting.

Finally, we should note that the Greek term *idios* is used in the New Testament pertaining to something belonging or being related to oneself in distinction to public property or what belongs to someone else; the word can be used by itself to indicate *one's own stuff*. Matthew 9:1, for example, identifies Jesus' *own* town or city (Capernaum). Acts 21:6 describes disciples returning, literally, to their *own possessions*, i.e., "home." Acts 4:32 describes the Jerusalem community as distinctive in that no one called anything *one's own*, no one claimed private ownership of any possessions.

An understanding of the term *idios* is important because it can be used without *oikos* or *oikia* to refer to one's own domicile or household as well as possessions.

We have examined these Greek terms because, in the absence of any exact equivalence of our concepts of home and family, these are the words whose usage is most likely to give us insight into the "family" in the world of Jesus. Further, Greek was an important part of the language world of Jesus. Some of Jesus' disciples were Greek; we know Philip was Greek because of his name, and in John 12:20–21 Diaspora Jews — Greek-speaking Jews living outside Judea who would not have spoken Hebrew or Aramaic — approach Philip for an audience with Jesus. Jesus preached in the Decapolis, "Ten Cities," a largely Greek-speaking area. And the occasions when Jesus used Aramaic are explicitly annotated in the New Testament, which suggests that he ordinarily used Greek. Although Rome was the dominant political entity, Rome had conquered a world in which Greek was already the *lingua franca* for commerce, education, government, and, even in Jewish communities outside Judea, for worship. Highly educated Jews like Philo of Alexandria were unlikely to speak or read Hebrew, and the Septuagint was the ordinary Bible of non-Judean Jews.

Trying to understand ancient texts is hard work, and we must make every effort to avoid assimilating ancient values to our contemporary ones. For one example of this, look at the frequent translations and insertions of "home" into Today's English Version. The 1611 King James Version consistently renders the Greek words *oikos/oikia* as "house." In subsequent translations, the word "home" appears more frequently, culminating in the TEV which also adds the word "home" without warrant into the English text. Matthew 2:12 reports that the magi "returned to their own country," whereas the TEV narrates, "They went back home by another road." According to TEV at Luke 8:27, the Gerasene demoniac "would not stay at home but spent his time in a cave." (We have seen that rural caves could *be* "home.") The NRSV says of the Gerasene demoniac that "he did not live in a house but in the tombs," indicating a contrast, lost to the TEV, between a civilized (pure) and an uncivilized (impure) abode. Similarly, in Luke 23:56, the women from Galilee go "back home" — but this cannot be to Galilee, because they are already staying in Jerusalem (23:49). As these examples indicate, introducing "home" into the TEV results in the imposition of contemporary understandings of privacy on ancient texts.

Houses in Ancient Rome and Palestine

All New Testament writings arose in a context of Roman law and society, and the descriptions of values at the time of Jesus originally operated within a Roman context. While Greek dominated the linguistic world of Jesus, the ruling political force was Rome, and archeology shows us the extent to which Roman legal and social mores influenced even ordinary households throughout the Roman Empire. The Latin word *familia,* while it has given us our modern word "family," was rarely used in the sense of kin. It could signify a collection of slaves attached singly or collectively to husband and wife, as well as freed slaves who bore the family name of their former owner to whom they owed life-long obligations (Seneca, Epistle 47, 14). *Familia* in legal contexts of property and inheritance identifies a *paterfamilias* (father of the *familia*) usually upon the death of his own father. Sometimes *familia* connotes the estate. When Romans wished to speak of lineage or kinship unit, they spoke of the "house" (Latin *domus*).

What do we know about these houses, homes, and estates at the time of Jesus? In Roman domestic architecture in Italy there seems to have been no separate spaces for men and women. The large open atrium, which had in pre-Roman times been the place where the mother of the family lived and executed such matronly tasks as spinning and weaving and directing her household, by Roman times had become the main room of the house. The center of the atrium was open to the sky, admitting light; a shallow pool

under the roof opening collected rainwater. In the atrium guests
and clients assembled every morning before their daily meeting
with the head of the household. The household deities resided
in the atrium, and a newly married couple would be symbolically
bedded there, recalling the ancient use of the room. Tradition-
ally most household tasks, including the tutoring of children and
maintenance of accounts, were performed there. In households
where slaves assumed many of these tasks, often moving them
out of the atrium, the Roman *matrona* continued to fulfill her
traditional role by weaving there, although she moved freely. A
Roman woman could own property, slaves, and commercial busi-
nesses that she could generally control without spousal approval.
She could attend public baths and participate in public events.

A Roman household underwent changes and could span generations; an aged parent might live with a husband and wife
together with their children. It might also include day laborers,
single relations staying for a time, married children residing until
they were part of their own nuclear household or had children
of their own. Slaves and children adopted by the *paterfamilias*,
slave children who shared the same nurse with the master's free
children, freedmen or foster children related to the family, or
foundlings, either free or slave (*alumni*) might also be included.
Scholar Beryl Rawson, however, envisages the great majority of
the population in Rome, and perhaps other towns and cities, living in small cramped apartments that had little space for more
than the conjugal family and a small number of slaves. For
such people, the neighborhood offered a significant wider space
and set of relationships; people who, were they more affluent,
would receive the public in their atria, instead went out into their
neighborhoods and thus extended the household into the street,
reversing the pattern of the wealthy household.

Roman architecture appears in both rural and urban settings
in Palestine alongside buildings from the earlier Hellenistic period and housing indigenous to the area, like the beehive houses

found in Syria. Nomadic populations lived in tents, and caves provided simple functional housing in the country. In locales where there were raw materials, workers in those materials lived in small workshops called *officinae*. Isolated farmhouses would have been common in rural areas. The well-excavated archeological site at Ramat Hanadiv includes structures from several periods, including a Phoenician shrine, a Herodian farmhouse, three winepresses, a Byzantine *villa rustica,* a Hellenistic village, a Herodian palace, and several Bronze Age tumuli. Pictures of rural Palestine also reveal the lack of tall trees, which placed constraints upon the size of any individual roofed construction. So in Palestine large gatherings took place outside or in courtyards, which, as in Rome, might be within or immediately adjacent to the house.

Most of the Palestinian houses mentioned in the New Testament, including those that Jesus dwelt in or visited, were urban houses, whether in small urban settings like villages, or larger ones such as towns and cities. The poor often lived in small one-room houses or houses that might have had two rooms if there was a second floor within; it is often difficult to ascertain the division of a structure into two floors. Households who rented or owned shops often lived in a dwelling attached to or above those shops. Some households might have lived in the back of and on a balcony above row shops. Hilly areas would mandate terrace houses sharing common walls that helped support each other. The most common urban house, however, was a house with a small side courtyard, several interior rooms and often two floors. Frequently the courtyards of several of these houses abutted on each other, forming a large common courtyard merging private and public spaces. The flat roofs of all dwellings provided additional living space, further merging public and private.

Larger Palestinian houses held central courtyards similar to Roman houses, with smaller rooms informally organized surrounding the courtyard. The households that inhabited Roman and Palestinian dwellings were similarly constituted, and it is to these we now turn.

Roman and Palestinian Households

The family as we know it today consists of parents and children, with extended family members such as grandparents, aunts, and uncles residing in their own houses. The ancient household in Roman, Greek, and Jewish settings was a far more inclusive unit, and people joined these households through adoption, slavery, and client status. Further, each of the familiar roles like father, mother, and child was shaped in ways sufficiently different from ours that they deserve examination. The ancient household also was the source for the economic societies known as guilds.

Slavery was normative in the world of Jesus' time and continued into the Byzantine period, enduring not simply because the economy depended upon it but because the concept of slavery itself was universally acknowledged and accepted. Slaves themselves acknowledged and supported this condition. Of course, there were different kinds of slaves, or *douloi,* including those who worked in agriculture as well as domestic slaves; on a large estate, there might well have been hundreds of slaves. But in a Roman *domus* (household, house) several slaves would be considered part of the *familia.*

Legally, slaves belonged to the *familia* in two ways: they were under the power of their masters, and they were owned. Their inferior position was deemed natural in the way a child is dependent on parents. Because they were property, slaves could be beaten or killed. When Seneca, a wealthy Roman senator, Stoic philosopher, and advisor to Nero, describes a simple life, it includes taking a few slaves (Seneca, Epistle 87, 2). To be sure, he sees slaves as more than property and advises living on friendly terms with them, "treating inferiors as you would be treated by your betters" (Epistle 47, 11). A well-run household is thought commendable and includes respect for slaves. Speaking to heads of households, Seneca (*On Anger* 3, 25, 3) counsels attending to larger and more important matters, such as patience and endurance, rather than trivial questions of whether your slaves, your freedman, your wife, or your clients answer you back or laugh in your household in the presence of the *paterfamilias.* "You should," he says, "lend ear to laughter and weeping, to soft words and bitter, to happiness and sorrow, to the voices of men and shouts of slaves."

Domestic slaves were entrusted with various tasks: wet nurses fed babies; *paedagogi,* often elder slaves, oversaw the protection and basic education of the house's children. Personal secretaries existed in wealthy households. Of all slaves, whether trained or untrained, *pietas,* namely, fidelity and loyalty to the household and its master, was expected. Freed persons worked alongside household slaves, but they had more privileges, such as the ability to enter into business contracts, marry, and leave property to their legitimate children born to free mothers. Investigation of Roman domestic architecture shows the ubiquitous presence of slaves such as nurses, tutors (*paedagogi*), and grooms throughout the house. It seems as though slaves had no independent space, although slaves would naturally be found in kitchens and stables. Historian Michele George points out that the key to understanding the absence of physical segregation is the psychological segregation: Romans could ignore the presence of slaves even in the most private of circumstances. We can only conjecture about the effects of this attitude on household dynamics.

A variety of children inhabited the household: those under the jurisdiction of a *paterfamilias* could be related by blood or marriage, could be legitimate or illegitimate, half-sibling or step-sibling, or have no kin ties at all. Sons and daughters of the upper classes might live in a variety of households, and siblings often lived apart from one another. A person who had married and given birth might expect to see a growing number of brothers and sisters well into adulthood.

In some ways, children were like slaves in that legally they were subject to the rule of the *paterfamilias.* The duty of a good parent, Seneca counsels (*On Mercy* 1, 14), is, like that of a good prince, to reprove children sometimes gently, sometimes with threats, and sometimes even by beatings. But no one resorts to punishment until all other means of correction have been exhausted. He regards training children in the same light as training animals. Children must not be allowed to have tantrums. As Quintilian argued, the whipping of students is bad pedagogy since it leads to a servile character. Following the mean implies that sometimes the child must be held back and sometimes encouraged. Boys in particular are raised to be respectful, law-abiding, and self-controlled adults. They cannot have unrestricted freedom since an unbearable character will result: "If a child has been given everything he asked for, if his anxious mother always comforted him when he cried, if his child-minder always let him do what he wanted, then he will never be able to cope with anything unpleasant in his life" (Seneca, *On Anger* 21, 1–6). Thus, we may take it that beatings of children and slaves were not uncommon.

Seneca was a wealthy Roman living near the capital. In the Roman provinces during the first five centuries of the Common Era, domestic slavery predominated over agricultural, particularly in cities like Alexandria and Antioch. What impact on household relations did slaves have? Seneca's remarks on child rearing indicate that parenting was shared between slaves and parents. What effect might relationships between children and their tutors have had on parent-child relations?

Within Roman households, women had the same physical and legal status as slaves and children. Imperial Roman wives could own property, but this was not true of Roman matrons during the late Republic. The same holds true of the household of the first-century writer Philo. Building on its biblical foundation in Exodus 20:12 and Deuteronomy 5:16, Philo understands the creation of children by their parents to be analogous to the creation of the world by God. According to Roman law, slaves and children were economically dependent on the father/master until they were manumitted, in the case of slaves, or in the case of children, came of age. In the Hellenistic Jewish story *Joseph and Asenath,* Asenath declares in her dedicatory prayer to God that she will be to Joseph a servant and a slave. While wives and slaves, unlike children, entered a house as outsiders, the sexual availability of slaves distinguished them from wives, whose chastity preserved the honor and authority of the head of the household.

Within a Roman household, mothers had influence over their daughters and, particularly if their father died, over their sons. But a woman's independent wealth was its own form of power. Julius Caesar had his mother living with him in his home with the implication that this was perhaps because of her wealth. Such a mother gave advice on who her son would marry. Thus a woman's power over her children differs from that of a man: hers is coercive while his is punitive.

Adoption

Adoption was widespread. In Galatians 4:6 Paul speaks of new members of the Galatian community as adopted sons who, having received a spirit of adoption, now call God "Abba, Father." In modern society, adoption is reserved to mean the bringing of infants or children into an exclusive binding legal relationship with one or more nonbiological parents. In the Roman world, while adoption of underage orphans could and did function like the fostering of young children for the purpose of nurturing and education, there was a far more important legal purpose for adoption. The adoption of adults was a standard means for the transmission of family property and continuation of a family name. As Augustus said, it was dishonorable for the estate of a family line to pass out of the family; therefore there were often cases where it was imperative to bring in some family. The status of the legally adopted heir was equal with, and in some cases overrode, the status of a biological descendent, if the testator so chose. Being a member of the family was about inheriting. A biological son or daughter who brought shame upon the family could be disinherited in favor of an adoptive heir; such disinheritance deprived the son or daughter not just of future hopes of property, but of any claim on family ties. This drastic disciplinary measure required public justification, demonstrating the extent to which family life was not a private matter as it is in our time. Conversely, while non-family members might be named as recipients of token legacies, inheriting was reserved to members of the family; Paul wrote to the Galatians as a Roman citizen speaking to a community living under Roman law, and the testamentary implications of this adoption as sons of God must not be overlooked when we consider Paul's theology about the family.

A parallel social group to that of the family is the association, or guild. Of the social groupings that existed in the world of Jesus' time, it is one of the most important for us to understand. A well-preserved stele found *in situ* in the southeast corner of the harbor area at Ephesus of Neronian date (54–59 CE) is evidence of a fishing cartel in first-century Ephesus. The stele lists over eighty-nine donors whose names identify a large group who had built a customs house for fishery toll at their own expense. Fishing guilds existed wherever this industry had become established on a basis involving more than two families. However, they might not exist everywhere: Luke 5:7 describes fishing business partners (*metochoi*), and 5:10 speaks of "partners, sharers" (*koinonoi*) assisting each other as need arises. Names on the Ephesus stele identify a range in civic status from Roman citizens to slaves, so it provides an intriguing look at the wide spread in rank attested of Pauline communities. We may conclude that the partners (i.e., families) of Peter and Andrew, James and John were not indigent or illiterate, but owned boats and fishing equipment. While there is no compelling reason to assume that they belonged to a fishing cartel, each family — the sons of Jonah and the sons of Zebedee — was able to release a son for a three-year period. This may have implications for Pauline mission: did Paul focus his attention on Roman citizens so that his adherents would possess enough wealth to host gatherings in their own homes? We could also ask whether the focus on Peter's role in Gentile mission at Acts 15:7 has something to do with his social and economic status as a fisherman already part of an association on the basis of familial affinity. It is important to note that as Luke 5:7 attests, two groups of brothers form an association. Perhaps the association was a second home.

Evidence within associations and diverse guilds in the Greco-Roman world from Greece and Asia Minor, as well as papyri from Egypt suggest that familial language was used among the members of these groups. Fellow members are referred to as "brothers" and, less frequently, "sisters"; leaders are called "mothers," "fathers," or even "papas." For example, the "sacred, athletic, wandering, world-wide association" professional guild of athletes devoted to the God Herakles moved its headquarters from Asia Minor to Rome around 143 CE. From the time of Constantine, members of this association expressed relations to each other using family metaphors such as "our brother" and "our father." Thus the values of such groups and associations — including brotherly love — are similar to the community values that are esteemed in New Testament writings. The idea of "family" extended far beyond parents, children, and blood relatives.

This sketch of family life at the time of Jesus includes an understanding of the *oikos* as a place of social and public identity. In the charts at the end of this book we can see the range of this word and related words in the New Testament. We need to resist reading modern European and Western assumptions about a secluded and private "home" back into ancient texts. An ancient household depended on *size:* it might include master, mistress, biological and adopted children, relatives, freedmen and women, foster children, slaves, their children, and land. And as we will see in the following chapter, the four Gospels offer very different pictures of Jesus' family life — different from one another and contrary to what we might expect.

Chapter Two

THE HOLY FAMILY

A BEAUTIFUL ICON of the Holy Family called *The Flight into Egypt* shows Mary holding the infant Jesus on her lap. She and the child are riding on a donkey to safety in Egypt while Joseph walks behind. It can be seen in the Coptic Museum in Cairo, Egypt, and in other Coptic churches and holy places up and down the Nile. The type is well known, and examples of it by artists from Giotto to Rembrandt exist in European and North American galleries. The Egyptian examples, however, have the advantage of being seen *in situ,* that is, in the very places the Holy Family are believed to have visited on their sojourn in Egypt. The second- or third-century Coptic Acts of Mark describes this journey of Jesus to Egypt and connects the Apostle Mark with the founding of Christianity in Egypt. Today the Coptic Church in Egypt maintains this tradition. Since 2000, tourists to Egypt have been able to consult maps and trace the route outlining the visit of the Holy Family to Egypt from Israel. The route into Egypt passes through Sinai and continues down the river Nile as far as Assiut. Places and buildings along their journey are marked and venerated as rest stops where the Holy Family ate, drank, or spent the night.

There is a sense of relief about this icon. Mary holds the child protectively. She and Joseph have escaped from Herod's murder of the "innocents," males under the age of two. The expressions on all faces are quite happy; the only figure that looks tired or over-burdened is the donkey. The clothes are rich and well decorated;

Jesus is waving his arms about as one would expect a two-year-old to do. The image also conveys the miraculous; that any child has survived Herod's slaughter of the innocents by strong, powerful men is extraordinary. Palms appear in the icon, and, with the donkey, seem to prefigure the triumphal entry into Jerusalem at the end of Jesus' life.

Only Matthew's and Luke's Gospels describe Jesus' birth. Matthew's Holy Family in Egypt survives Herod's death threat thanks to foreign hospitality. In this way, Matthew prefigures Jesus' hostile treatment at the hands of those who should have known their scriptures better. Let's look at Mathew's story first, in which Joseph is warned of Herod's threats against the child Jesus and instructed by the angel to take the child and his mother to Egypt for safety, thus fulfilling Hosea 11:1, "Out of Egypt have I called my son." What is interesting here are the angel's words of warning to Joseph in Matthew 2:13, which identify the "Holy Family" as "the child and his mother." These words are echoed by the narrative in 2:14, "Then Joseph got up, took *the child and his mother* by night and went to Egypt," where they remain until Herod dies. Then, after Herod's death, Joseph takes "the child and his mother" (2:21) from Egypt into Galilee. Is this not a strange description of Jesus, Mary, and Joseph? While viewers of the icon might see Joseph (husband), Mary (wife), and Jesus (their child), three times Matthew describes "the child and his mother" as distinct from Joseph for the simple reason that Joseph is not the father of the child. What does this phrase signify about the Holy Family?

The genealogy with which Matthew opens the Gospel establishes Jesus' patrilineal ancestry through male ancestors, including David and Abraham. Each ancestor generates, or "begets," a son who in turn generates another for three groups of fourteen generations until "Jacob begat Joseph" (1:16). Then exactly at the point a reader might expect to find "Joseph begat Jesus," there is a shift: Joseph is identified as the "husband" of Mary. The generating verb then becomes passive: " . . . Mary, *of whom Jesus was born,* who is called the Messiah." Joseph does not "beget" Jesus, nor is he Jesus' father. The genealogy connects Jesus to his male ancestors through Mary alone. Therefore when Joseph names Jesus as the angel commanded, he becomes Jesus' adoptive father.

Matthew's genealogy links Jesus to certain male ancestors, including David and Abraham, through Joseph and his marriage to Mary. Yet at the same time, Jesus has only one father in Matthew's Gospel: the heavenly Father. Jesus teaches the disciples to pray "Our Father" in the Lord's Prayer. This is "the one in the heavens," not on earth. Matthew's community is one in which members are siblings, that is, children of the heavenly Father. Furthermore, this affiliation is exclusive: Jesus admonishes his followers: "Call no one father on earth, for you have one Father, the one in heaven" (23:9). Joseph's role in the opening chapters of the Gospel, however, is crucial because the child's life is threatened. The first thing the Gospel says of Joseph is that he is "a just person" (1:19), not first and foremost a father. While he is thinking about divorcing Mary secretly, not wishing to shame her publicly, an angel of the Lord asks him to contemplate an act of higher righteousness going beyond the Law: to marry Mary and adopt the child as his son by naming him Jesus. All this Joseph does without demurral. He obeys the angel and takes "the child and his mother" to safety in Egypt.

It is Joseph's righteous deed, not his family ties, that saves the life of the child. After the death of Herod, Joseph brings the child and his mother back into Israel. Exercising his own judgment, Joseph avoids the threat of Herod's son Archelaus ("like father, like son"), and dwells in Nazareth. He is thus a model parent caring for those in his household to whom he is not biologically related. In Joseph's compassion and foresight for his adoptive child and care for the child's mother, Matthew's portrait of Joseph anticipates those of other caring parents and heads of households in the Gospel, all of whom request something of Jesus on behalf of those in their care or households: a centurion for his slave (8:6), a ruler of the synagogue for his daughter (9:18), the Canaanite woman for her child (15:22), the mother of the sons of Zebedee for her sons (20:21). Moreover, Joseph's conduct toward a child not his own contrasts with Herod's malevolence toward children in his kingdom. A king ought to have compassion for children of his realm, but the slaughter of the innocents was credible because Herod was known to have executed three of his own sons and exemplifies the anti-type of father. As I will show in chapter 3, Matthew displaces earthly fathers in favor of the one heavenly Father, but the Gospel goes to great length to commend appropriate and to condemn inappropriate parental conduct within the Matthean community. Joseph behaves toward the child and his mother in the way that a law-abiding righteous individual would do in the singular dilemma in which he finds himself. A centurion requests that Jesus heal a slave of his household. A leader of the synagogue requests that Jesus bring his daughter back to life. A Canaanite woman, perhaps herself a slave proselyte, asks for healing for her daughter. But the aggrandizing request of the mother of the sons of Zebedee is not Jesus' to grant.

Thus, icons of the Holy Family in Egypt viewed through the Gospel lens depict not husband, wife, and their child, but rather mother and child together with adoptive father. On the surface, this looks like a nuclear family. Yet at the same time as the image constructs, it also deconstructs the Holy Family. What looks like father, mother, and child both is and is not what it seems: it may look like "father, mother, and child" but is in fact "Joseph, the child, and his mother."

Christian texts after the New Testament continue this idea of distance between Joseph and "the child and his mother." The stability of this theme indicates the influence of the biblical narrative. A good example can be found in the Gospel of Pseudo-Matthew, a narrative incorporating oral stories as well as additions to the biblical account of Jesus' birth. Dating perhaps from the eighth or ninth century CE, many copies of this text exist, confirming its influence in art and popular devotion. It records that on the third day of their journey, overcome with heat, Mary tells Joseph that she wishes to rest in the shade of a date palm. Noticing the tree full of fruit, Mary declares, "I wish someone could get me some of the fruits of the palm tree." Joseph responds, "I wonder that you say this, for you see how high this palm tree is, and (I wonder) that you even think about eating of the fruits of the palm. I think rather of the lack of water, which already fails us in the skins, and we have nothing with which we can refresh ourselves and the animals." Jesus, however, commands the tree to bend down its branches and refresh his mother with its fruit. The tree obliges and, at a further command from Jesus, opens a vein of water by its roots in the form of a fountain that refreshes the thirst of human and animal alike. On the journey through Egypt, according to Pseudo-Matthew, it is the child Jesus rather than an unsympathetic Joseph who responds to his mother Mary's needs — a detail that emphasizes the distance between "the child and his mother" and Joseph.

This story from Pseudo-Matthew has much in common with the popular "Cherry Tree Carol," which may have derived from Pseudo-Matthew. Here the date becomes a cherry, which Joseph not only refuses to pluck for Mary, but responds in a way that impugns the purity of Mary: "Let the one who got you with child, pluck you the cherry." The two may date from a similar time, so it is hard to determine which version of the story is original. Is Pseudo-Matthew painting Joseph in a more favorable light in correction of the carol, or is the "Cherry Tree Carol" elevating Mary in response to Pseudo-Matthew? In both cases, the texts presume tension between husband and wife.

Matthew's Gospel identifies Jesus as the descendent of Abraham and David through the genealogy of chapter 1, and where he comes from through involuntary and voluntary geographical moves in chapter 2. The Holy Family goes from Bethlehem of Judea to Egypt; from Egypt to Israel; and finally within Israel to

Nazareth in Galilee. Each place is named and sanctioned by a citation from prophetic scripture: this happened to fulfill the words of the prophet Hosea, or Micah, or Jeremiah, or the prophets. In Matthew, prophetic scripture identifies place and event: Jesus fulfills Hosea's prophecy "Out of Egypt have I called my son" by being brought to Egypt in the arms of his mother through the agency of Joseph. Fleeing political threats, the refugees move from place to place as transients. Yet in this narrative Matthew describes Bethlehem and Nazareth as more permanent locations. Born in a house in Bethlehem of Judea to fulfill the prophecy of Micah 5:2, the child is surrounded with wealthy gifts from foreign dignitaries. After sojourning in Egypt to fulfill Hosea 11:1, Jesus and his mother are eventually taken by Joseph to Nazareth "to fulfill that which was spoken by the prophets: 'He shall be called of Nazareth'" (Tyndale's translation).

All translations of Matthew agree that the wise men visit Jesus in a house (2:11); no stable exists in Matthew. The stable or manger is in Luke and in medieval legends like those of the Gospel of Pseudo-Matthew, where Luke's story is harmonized with Matthew's by Mary's placing Jesus in the manger between two animals three days after his birth. What sort of a building is Matthew's house? Illustrations of Matthew's Adoration of the Magi in Western Christian art interpret the house as large: the wise men present their gifts to the child and his mother under a roof, sometimes without walls, or in front of an open building with walls and a roof. Whatever Matthew understood by the *oikos* as a location for Jesus' birth, painters (correctly, in my opinion) in Western Christian art depict it as a *public* not a private house, large enough to accommodate foreign dignitaries and their retinues. Large Roman or Palestinian houses exist in first-century Galilee with public and private spaces. If we think of Matthew's *oikos* as a large house with both public and private rooms, an audience with a large assemblage of visitors from the East is conducted in public, not private, space.

Luke's "Extended Family"

Matthew's account of Jesus' birth highlights the protecting role of Joseph, whereas in Luke Joseph is known only as the husband of Mary and a descendent of David. In Matthew, Joseph receives the dream that will save the child and his mother from Herod's massacre of the children. Matthew's depiction of the Holy Family differs from Luke's focus on Elizabeth and Mary, mothers of John the Baptist and Jesus. The relationship these two kinswomen have with each other connects Luke's stories of the birth of John and Jesus, while their husbands, Zechariah and Joseph, are for the most part silent. But in Matthew, Joseph is the righteous law-abiding individual whose actions save the child and his mother. That he recognizes a child not born to him means that he brings the Holy Family into being. He models the care of a *paterfamilias* for those in his household.

In Luke's birth stories, on the other hand, an extended family constellation emerges that is very different from Matthew's "nuclear family." More people are involved. John the Baptist and Jesus are born at about the same time to women who are related to each other, and these women are the focus of Luke's story: "In the sixth month [of Elizabeth's pregnancy] the angel Gabriel was sent by God to a town in Galilee called Nazareth." Jesus' mother becomes pregnant six months into Elizabeth's pregnancy. Both pregnancies are a surprise. Elizabeth has been barren and thus dishonored; now past the age of childbearing, she and her husband Zechariah still long for a child. Mary is engaged to Joseph with whom she fully expects to have children in due course. In contrast to Matthew, Joseph is mentioned only to identify him as of Davidic lineage and as the fiancé of Mary. John's father, Zechariah, on the other hand, belongs to the priestly order of Abijah and is serving in the Jerusalem Temple, while his mother is a descendent of Aaron, brother of Moses.

An angel of the Lord appears first to Zechariah to announce that his wife Elizabeth is pregnant with a son who is to be named

John. He will be filled with the Holy Spirit and will turn many in Israel to the Lord, their God. Zechariah queries the angel: "How will I know that this is so? For I am an old man and my wife is getting on in years." For his temerity, Gabriel identifies himself and declares that Zechariah will be unable to speak until such time as the prophecy is fulfilled. Perhaps Zechariah is punished because he knows the stories of Hebrew scriptures in which God opens and closes wombs of elderly faithful women like Sarah. Whatever the reason, the silence of Zechariah propels Elizabeth and Mary into center stage: Elizabeth indeed becomes pregnant and remains in seclusion for five months, perhaps to safeguard the pregnancy or perhaps until the pregnancy becomes obvious.

Gabriel then appears to a virgin named Mary. Actually her name in the Greek text is Mariam, the Greek name for Miriam, which evokes a connection with Miriam, the Hebrew prophet. She is not terrified but puzzled by the angel's greeting. Gabriel reassures her as he reassured Zechariah: she will soon become pregnant with a son whom she will name Jesus. Jesus is to be called Son of the Most High, and he will be rule an endless kingdom from the throne of his ancestor David. Like Zechariah, Mary queries the angel: "How can this be, since I am a virgin?" The angel's response to Mary is sympathetic rather than angry: he explains that the power of the Most High will overshadow her and that the child to be born will be called Son of God. As proof of this promise, she is told that Elizabeth her kinswoman is six months pregnant. Mary accepts the angel's prophecy and goes at once to the house of Zechariah where she finds the pregnant Elizabeth. At Mary's greeting, Elizabeth's child jumps within her womb for joy and Elizabeth utters a beatitude to Mary: "Blessed is the woman who believed that there would be a completion of what had been spoken to her by the Lord." The two stories of John and Jesus converge when the two pregnant kinswomen greet each other in the well-known scene of the Visitation, recognizing with mutual affection and joy the evidence of their pregnancies.

It is possible but unlikely that Gabriel's announcement of a coming pregnancy is predicated on normal sexual relations with Joseph after they are married. The text notes that Mary is a virgin and she describes herself as such. Mary herself, however, intuits that the pregnancy will take place immediately, *before* she has sexual relations with her husband. The pregnancy is obvious to John in the womb of Elizabeth shortly afterward as the baby leaps in recognition at the sound of Mary's greeting. Elizabeth is already six months pregnant when the Annunciation to Mary occurs. Mary remains with Elizabeth "about three months" after the visit, and yet she still leaves before John is born. Even if Luke thought of the term of a pregnancy as ten (lunar) months rather than nine, this still leaves a relatively short interval between the Annunciation and the Visitation. Perhaps it is best to take her query as a literary device created by Luke to enable the angel to explain specifics of the pregnancy to her. Why is Mary's incredulity tolerated when Zechariah's is not? Perhaps Zechariah is punished for his temerity because his situation has a precedent — the Torah account of Sarah's late pregnancy with Isaac, or Hannah's with Samuel. Mary is not punished for her question because her situation is without precedent. The angel's explanation answers her query. That she is not silenced for questioning, as was Zechariah, means that it is her song and not Zechariah's that is the first extended song of praise to God recorded in Luke.

When I visualize the Annunciation, it is da Vinci's rendering in the Uffizi Gallery in Florence that I see. Gabriel appears to interrupt Mary while she is reading Hebrew scriptures. Da Vinci's conceit belongs to a type of Annunciation scene showing Mary reading. Other types (e.g., Rogier van der Weyden) depict Mary kneeling at a prie-dieu. In my reading of da Vinci's *Annunciation,* Mary is reading Hebrew scriptures in the manner of a devout Jewish woman. This is how the Magnificat portrays God's mighty acts in Hebrew scriptures: God has shown strength with his arm, scattered the proud, regarded those of no consequence, put down the mighty from their thrones, and filled the hungry with good things. Her praise of God's actions is in concert with what she experiences as her own exaltation by God. After she gives birth to Jesus and presents him in Jerusalem as holy to the Lord, Simeon praises God for the birth of the child and predicts that this child "is destined for the falling and rising of many in Israel." To Mary he says, "a sword will pierce your soul also."

Significantly, neither account in the Gospels depicts an ordinary birth: in both, Mary's blameless pregnancy occurs before she has sexual relations with Joseph. Indeed it is Mary's singularity, the mode of her pregnancy and the manner of its disclosure, that marks her as unique. Even when Mary's conception and birth of Jesus is set alongside Elizabeth's birth of John, Mary's pregnancy is distinctive: marriage is the means of Elizabeth's pregnancy, but not of Mary's. That she gives birth without pain, and that, in the Catholic tradition, she is mother of only one child is further evidence of her singularity, especially in centuries before modern forms of family planning.

Luke's Holy Family, unlike Matthew's, centers on the means by which Mary, Jesus' mother, gives birth through the agency of the Holy Spirit. The whole story is presented as a parallel to Elizabeth's, a comparison which serves to show Jesus' birth in an even more extraordinary light. While Elizabeth's pregnancy follows the example in Hebrew scriptures of older women, like Sarah, becoming pregnant late in life, Mary's is unique. The effect of these parallel stories on Jesus' family of origin according to Luke serves to enlarge it so as to include the account of John's birth. Recognition and confirmation of Mary's pregnancy comes from the evidence of Elizabeth's own pregnancy; support for Mary in her condition comes not from her future husband but from seclusion with her kinswoman Elizabeth in her pregnancy. Luke's depiction of what we would call an extended family can be seen in Western Christian art. Mary, her child Jesus, and Joseph are shown either with John the Baptist alone or with John and Elizabeth, his mother. For example, Peter Paul Reubens depicts Mary supporting the baby Jesus on her lap; Jesus' left arm stretches toward another baby, John the Baptist, seated on Elizabeth's lap. Elizabeth is clearly elderly. Behind Mary in the top left corner of the painting stands a male figure in the background, probably Joseph, looking down toward Mary and to Elizabeth and her son beyond. The whole group, connected through the kinswomen, Mary and Elizabeth, and their children, Jesus and John, together with Mary's husband, Joseph (who is not Jesus' biological father), constitutes Luke's version of an extended Holy Family.

Matthew and Luke's Holy Families, however distinct from each other, both present families of origin that look at least superficially like families that we know today. When we turn to John's Gospel, we encounter something altogether different.

John: The Family at the Cross

There are no birth stories in John's Gospel. Instead we find ourselves in a strange place, namely, the beginning. The word "beginning" evokes creation and the start of Genesis, "When God began to create the heavens and the earth...." Like Genesis, the prologue to John's Gospel describes God's creation as speech; unlike Genesis, however, it personifies God's speech as *logos,* or Word: "In the beginning was the Word." Jesus as the *logos* of God exists as God's Word or Wisdom in the beginning, according to John. In fact, Jesus as *logos* is God's personified Word. Since the Word becomes flesh only in verse 14, much of John's prologue before that describes Jesus' preexistence, namely, where he was before he was born. No other Gospel describes Jesus' preexistence.

While John describes the *logos* bringing the world into being with God, the world fails to recognize the *logos*. John 1:10–11 clarifies a motif of rejection familiar from wisdom tradition: the world does not know him, and those who are his do not receive him. The NRSV translates verse 11 as: "He came to what was his own, and his own people did not accept him." A footnote renders an alternative translation: "He came to his own home..." (TEV proposes "his own country"). The Greek is a plural form of a substantive noun that can indicate home and possessions: literally, "one's own things." It occurs again at 19:27 when, from the cross, Jesus commands the beloved disciple to take Jesus' mother "to what was his own," i.e., "his home" (NRSV, RSV). What the NRSV translation is trying to reflect, it seems to me, is that while Jesus as *logos* is known and recognized by some for whom he has an affinity, *logos* is in fact "the one from heaven," namely, the preexistent Word, whose sojourn on earth is merely temporary. If Jesus is identified as God's Word in the beginning, then it is not surprising that familial relations in John are characterized not by closeness, but distance. Yet throughout the Gospel and at the end of his life Jesus creates from the cross a community of brothers, sisters, and friends as his last will and testament.

Although not all receive Jesus as the Word, those who do are given power to become children of God, born not of the will of the flesh or of blood or of human desire but of God. In John, the creation of God's children — that is, God's family — comes about without mothers and fathers, without any human agency. The whole Gospel explores how the family of God's followers come into being in a nonbiological way. Since the idea is complex, the Gospel tries different analogies to explain it. Thus John 1:12 describes the begetting of a family without human agency, without womb or sperm. In chapter 3 Nicodemus, who comes to Jesus by night, finds out what it means to be born "anew," from above. To be born from above or born anew does not mean entering into the mother's womb a second time but, as Jesus explains to a mystified Nicodemus, being born of water and the Spirit.

If John's Gospel describes the generation of families in a nonbiological way, one can see why Jesus' parents and his family of origin are unimportant. To be sure, Jesus has a mother, but he never addresses her as such. Except at Cana, neither of them makes claims on the other as family members or those in the same household might be expected to do, and even at Cana Mary's claim is not framed in terms of family obligation.

The distance between Jesus and his biological family can be seen in the complete absence of Joseph from John's Gospel. We have already noted the absence of a birth narrative. Joseph is not with Mary at the wedding in Cana. Those who identify Jesus as son of Joseph, and who claim to know his father and mother, are mistaken and fail to understand his true identity as "living bread, come down from heaven" (6:51). Jesus distances himself from the Jewish authorities by pointing out that "your fathers ate manna in the wilderness and died" (6:49). In John, Jesus' father is God: he often calls God "My Father"; however, Jesus calls his mother "Woman."

The two exchanges between Jesus and his mother take place at the beginning and end of the Gospel. In both stories, she is unnamed; in both stories, Jesus calls her "Woman." His words to her in Cana, "Woman, what have I to do with you?" (John 2:4), seem abrupt, even dismissive, if one assumes that filial relations with parents should be respectful. Even in Luke 2:51 Jesus is obedient to his parents after he has told them that he must be "attending to the things of his Father" or "be in my Father's house." But perhaps Jesus' words to his mother only seem abrupt to us; they do not seem to upset her. She says to the servants, "Do whatever he tells you" (2:5). At the end of the story, he remains in Capernaum with his mother and brothers for several days.

Jesus' words, "Woman, what have I to do with you?" may be seen alongside his words to his mother from the cross: "Woman, behold your son." In John's Gospel he tends to speak to women this way. To the Samaritan woman he says, "Woman, believe me . . ."; to the woman taken in adultery, "Woman, where are [your accusers]?"; and to Mary of Magdala, "Woman, why are you weeping?" With this mode of address Jesus as Son of God distances himself from his earthly mother and the other women with whom he converses. Moreover, he distances women from their men: to the Samaritan woman he says, "You are right in saying, 'I have no husband,' for you have had five husbands, and the one you have now is not your husband. What you have said

is true!" (4:17–18). In this Gospel parents also separate or differentiate themselves from their children; for example, the parents
of the man born blind say, "Ask him, he is of age" (9:23). Jesus
himself compares a woman forgetting the anguish of birth in the
joy of holding her child to the disciples' pain upon Jesus' departure — pain that will soon turn to joy (16:21–22). The disciples'
joy is one they will experience only after the departure of Jesus.

It is in keeping with this theme that in John the use of the word
"friend" replaces the language for family members and servants.
In John 15:13 Jesus identifies no greater love than to lay down
one's life for one's friends. His followers are no longer called
servants but friends because unlike servants or slaves who do not
know what their master is doing, Jesus' friends are those to whom
he has made known everything from the Father. Could "friend"
actually be a technical term replacing the language of family in
John's Gospel?

Standing near the cross toward the end of the Gospel are Jesus'
mother, her sister, and Mary Magdalene, while the other three
Gospels place Mary Magdalene first. Also distinctive to John's
crucifixion scene is the new relationship between his mother and
the beloved disciple, as Jesus gives her into John's care and thus
replaces himself as son to his mother. Affiliation is no longer
through birth, if it ever was; Jesus' mother is now mother or
guardian to the prototypical disciple in whatever community exists after Jesus' death. From the cross, in a last will and testament,
Jesus himself gives a new son to his mother, creating a mother-
son bond through his last words. The new son takes his new
mother into his realm (or house) and in so doing sustains the
bond. Through his words Jesus also creates a new family of his
disciples — the brothers, sisters, and friends that he loves, the most
prominent of whom becomes son to his mother. The beloved disciple is thus (re)born child of God not by desire, by procreation,
or by the will of the flesh.

Among this new kinship group continuing in the community
of the beloved disciple are women disciples, Mary of Magdala,

and Mary the wife of Clopas (who may be his aunt). In his appearance to Mary Magdalene at the tomb, Jesus commands her, "Go to my brothers and say to them, 'I am ascending to my Father and your Father, to my God and your God'" (20:17). At this moment he identifies Mary and his disciples as a family with a shared Father, their God, who becomes explicitly the father of the Johannine community. Up until now, Jesus has referred to God only as "my Father" or "the Father," not "your Father." Mary of Magdala now becomes Jesus' sibling. Thus, John's Gospel brings family groupings into being without flesh, womb, or human desire. From the cross and in the garden, a dying or resurrected Jesus creates his or others' new family by means of a word. Such creative speech echoes the language of the opening chapter.

In the early seventeenth century Peter Paul Reubens painted the Johannine Holy Family. Entitled *Christ on the Cross,* the painting shows a crucified Christ with open mouth inclining his head to the right so as to communicate with Mary and the beloved disciple. Mary collapses on the ground, her side pierced by a sword. But she is held by the right hand of John resting on her shoulder while he looks toward Christ to hear his words. While apostles Peter and Mary Magdalene occupy the left of the painting, our focus is on the newly constituted family group on the right: a crucified Jesus whose open mouth speaks his last will and testament to John as the disciple supports his new mother.

Mark: Leaving Home and Abandoning Family

Less than halfway through Mark's Gospel, Jesus has to reassure the disciple Peter about the consequences of leaving home and family. Jesus has just told the rich young man what he needs to do to inherit eternal life — to sell everything and give to the poor. As the young man goes away shocked and grieving over this challenge, Peter reminds Jesus that he and the other disciples have become poor: "We have left everything and followed you." Jesus promises him, "Truly, I tell you, there is no one who has left house or brothers or sisters or mother or father or children or fields, for my sake and for the sake of the good news, who will not receive a hundredfold now in this age — houses, brothers and sisters, mothers, children and fields, with persecutions — and in the age to come, eternal life" (10:29–30).

This translation identifies *oikiai*, households, as property in a context of *agroi*, fields — the land that supplies a livelihood to members of the household. Would-be disciples of Jesus leave people behind in the house: brothers and sisters, mother and father and children (a wife is not mentioned), namely, three generations including parents, their adult children, and their siblings, some of whom have children. To argue, as some modern scholars do, that this separation is typical of Jesus' attitude to households, however, fails to do justice either to the entire context of Mark 10 or to the details of other passages from the Gospels.

Have the disciples left everything including families (and households) to follow Jesus?

The immediate context of Peter's observation in Mark 10:28, "Look, we have left everything and followed you," is the contrast between the reluctance of the rich man to follow Jesus' advice to sell all he has in order to attain the kingdom and the disciples' apparent abandonment of houses, siblings, parents, children, and fields "for the sake of the gospel." The rich man has already indicated his fulfillment of the commandments, including "Honor your father and mother." Jesus' answer presupposes that keeping the commandments puts one well on the way toward inheriting eternal life: "You lack one thing. . . ." We can safely construe from this that Jesus affirms the commandment to honor father and mother, and that he himself would have kept it.

To be sure, Jesus' response contrasts abandonment of households for the sake of the gospel with eternal life in the age to come. But his words to Peter promise receiving a hundredfold now in this age — houses, brothers and sisters, mothers and children, and fields. The absence of wives, husbands, or fathers from the restored community seems to imply that what replaces the original families in this age is a new community of households, both sociological and domestic, including siblings, mothers, and children. Perhaps the best way to take Peter's statement, "Look, we have left everything and followed you," is not so much hyperbole as descriptive of a temporary state. Jesus' response acknowledges that disciples have at this moment left households and livelihoods, but that disciples will receive recompense (with persecutions) in the present age rather than in the distant future. The recompense is this new community.

Something similar may be seen in Luke's description of the calling of Levi (5:27–29). Seeing Levi sitting at a tax booth, Jesus says to him, "Follow me." The text records that Levi got up, left everything, and followed him. Then, the text continues, "Levi gave a great banquet for him in his house; and there was a large crowd of tax collectors and others sitting at table with them." It is obvious that Levi has not left "everything" or he would not be able to host a great banquet for Jesus in his house. Several translations (NRSV, TEV) attempt to alleviate the problem by creating a new paragraph before mention of Levi's great banquet for Jesus. However, Luke's statement that he "left everything" should perhaps be taken as hyperbole, exaggeration, since Levi has left everything and followed him just for the space between verses 28 and 29!

An added feature of the call of Levi, and what exactly he gave up to follow Jesus, is Luke's ambiguous attitude to wealth and possessions. In his Gospel Mary sings of God's power to raise the lowly and bring down the mighty from their thrones in the Magnificat, and Jesus' first sermon at Nazareth proclaims his ministry of preaching to the poor and freeing prisoners. However, Luke's inclusion of stories about a rich fool, or Zacchaeus, or a good Samaritan, or a prodigal son indicates his sympathy for the wealthy as long as they do not store up treasures for themselves but are rich toward God (12:21). Thus riches *per se* are not bad. After all, rich women, including Mary Magdalene, Joanna, and Susanna, financially underwrite Jesus and his disciples out of their resources (Luke 8:1–3). Moreover, as Clement of Alexandria notes in his second-century treatise "Who Is the Rich Man That Shall Be Saved?" one cannot shelter the homeless or feed the poor if one has nothing to offer. The good Samaritan demonstrates neighborliness precisely by paying the innkeeper to take care of the person who had fallen among thieves, something an indigent itinerant would have been unable to do.

But perhaps it is Luke's contribution to the discussion to note simply that disciples have not, in fact, left everything to follow Jesus, and that being well off is not grounds for automatic exclusion from discipleship. Mark's contribution, as noted, is to promise recompense in this age, rather than very soon. So we may take it that following Jesus for some disciples meant a temporary absence from previous occupations, such as fishing, to which they returned after Jesus' death. Rather than imagining discipleship as itinerant ministry of no fixed abode, it seems likely that Mark's Gospel locates Jesus' and the disciples' ministries moving between others' houses in Galilee and Jesus' own home in Capernaum, primarily in small towns, that is, in urban, not rural settings.

Some translations render Mark 2:1 thus: "it was reported that [Jesus] was at home." Exercising caution about the preference of modern translations for "home," I prefer Tyndale's reading: "it was noysed that he was in a housse." Whose house is this? The only previous house mentioned in Capernaum is the house of Simon and Andrew. While the house of Mark 2:1 may not be Jesus' house, Matthew concurs with Mark in identifying Capernaum as Jesus' home base. Although the prepositional phrase *en oiko* can have the connotation "at home," the particular passage ought to be understood in the context of the whole Gospel.

It is striking that in the earlier chapters of Mark, Jesus enters houses whose owners are not clearly identified, such as the house of Levi. After chapter 10, furthermore, houses belong to other people (the house of Simon the leper in Bethany) or have a technical meaning (the "house of God," namely, the Jerusalem Temple). Later Jesus has a guest room in Jerusalem where he eats the Passover with his disciples, so he is not "at home" in or near Jerusalem. He is at home in Capernaum, either in his house or staying in other's houses in a manner similar to the disciples' charge: "Whenever you enter a house, stay there until you leave the place" (6:10). In none of these cases can we be absolutely sure that Jesus owns a house or that such a house is his home.

An earlier story in Mark's Gospel introduces the notion of "family" in a very ambiguous way. Immediately after Jesus' appointing of the twelve disciples, the NRSV tells us, "Then he went home; and the crowd came together again, so that they could not even eat. When his family heard it, they went out to restrain him, for people were saying, 'He has gone out of his mind'" (3:19–21). But this translation as "family" rests, I fear, on an insecure foundation. Both the King James Version and Tyndale's translation describe the same group differently — as "they that longed unto him," "friends," or "kinsmen." The underlying Greek phrase should first be recognized as "his own" or "a group of his," the *idios* we examined in the first chapter. By extension, such a phrase can be translated as "family." But is that in fact correct? Can the phrase have another meaning? Where else does the phrase or something like it appear in Mark? Mark 1:36 refers to "Simon and his companions" with a similar phrase, identifying Andrew, James, and John. So perhaps the story in Mark 3:21 refers to a group of companions, disciples, not a family. What about the surrounding context?

If Jesus "went home," then perhaps the context suggests that "his own" who set out to restrain him in verse 21 is his family. If that is so, from where did they set out to restrain him? Were some "at home" and some not? But if *en oiko* simply means that Jesus went *into a house*, then perhaps "his own" in verse 21 are either the crowd (the immediate plural antecedent) or the twelve disciples who have just been called "to be with him" (3:14). If we take "a group of his" or "his own" as referring to the twelve, then they go with Jesus into a house and come out to restrain Jesus forcibly very soon after their selection. Perhaps Mark is emphasizing that the disciples are selected by Jesus and then immediately attempt to restrain him, in the same way that Judas is simultaneously appointed and identified as the one who "handed him over" or "betrayed" him (3:19).

If this is the case, then Jesus' mother and brothers are not introduced for the first time until later: "Then his brothers and his mother came; and standing outside, they sent to him and called him" (3:31). This is the first time we see them, standing outside and calling to him. Jesus does nothing to decrease their distance or move toward them. Responding to the observation of the crowd, "Your mother and your brothers and your sisters are outside asking for you," Jesus replies to those sitting around him in a circle, "Who are my mother and my brothers?" Here he identifies as brother, sister, and mother — family — those who do the will of God rather than those who are actually his kin. Thus Jesus identifies the crowd around him, those who do the will of God, as a family based on something besides consanguinity. The boundaries of this newly constituted familial group are permeable. Its membership includes brothers, sisters, and mothers, but not fathers. Only God is to be called Father.

Jesus' Family: Outsiders and Insiders

It is striking that soon after calling into being a new family of those who do the will of God, Jesus goes on to use the language of kinship in the context of two healing stories. Jairus, a leader of the synagogue, comes to Jesus and begs him to heal his small daughter, whose death is imminent. As Jesus goes with Jairus, he is followed by a woman "who had been suffering from hemorrhages for twelve years" — an ailment that excludes her from the religiously observant community. She makes her way through the press of the accompanying crowd, certain that if she manages to touch even Jesus' garment, she will be healed. She succeeds, and Jesus immediately recognizes the outflow of healing energy. He rounds on the crowd and asks, "Who touched me?" The disciples discount Jesus' question as silly, but the woman confesses publicly. He says to her, "Daughter, your faith has healed you" (5:34). By calling the woman "Daughter," Jesus, in effect, constructs a family of his own where there has been none before.

As he says this, emissaries from Jairus's house come up to notify Jairus of his daughter's death. Jesus reassures Jairus and continues toward his house, after dismissing everyone except Peter, James, and John. In the house, in the typical public open courtyard within the house, Jesus evicts all the professional mourners and goes further into the house, into a room, with the child's mother and father and his three disciples. He grasps the child's hand and tells her to get up. She obeys and walks around. The onlookers are amazed, and Jesus tells them to give her some food. In this story Jairus cannot heal his own daughter, but Jesus gives new life to an adult woman unrelated to him in response to a request from a father for his daughter.

How do oppositions and polarities work in the story to shape and reconfigure who is inside and outside a family? First, we note that this is not one but two stories, and they are set one inside the other. The inner story interprets the outer. Common vocabulary and themes connect the two stories: the request from both parties is made using the same Greek word for "saving," and both suppliants fall at Jesus' feet. Both women healed are called daughters, in one case a woman who has been ill for twelve years and in the other a girl who is twelve years old. Both are ritually unclean through either hemorrhaging or death. Touch is crucial to both healings: the woman touches Jesus' garment and Jesus grasps the little girl's hand. Finally, fear and faith are part and parcel of both stories.

The immediate effect of setting one story inside the other is that Jairus's daughter, who had been dying when her father first made the request, dies before Jesus' arrival perhaps because of the delay caused by the other suppliant's story. Salvation and healing for the inside story mean tragedy for the outside story. But in fact, salvation and healing is now extended in greater degree. The reader, like Jesus and Jairus, must ignore disparagers and servants who announce to him that his daughter is dead, must ignore and indeed expel from the house weeping, wailing, and commotion, must put aside scornful laughter, and above all, must not fear but only believe.

For the women, a change has taken place. For the older woman, telling "the whole truth" has made her healing permanent. Al though the little girl is effectively dead at the beginning of the episode, by the end of the episode she is touched by Jesus and called forth into life. We see her getting up and walking about. Moreover, she is now no longer identified as Jairus's daughter but acts independently. At the same time that Jairus's daughter separates from him, Jesus has gained a daughter.

Jesus himself has been changed by the episodes. At the beginning he is passive: he goes with the ruler of the synagogue to attend to his dying daughter. Before he reaches his patient, a woman in the crowd drains him of power by touching his garment. He reacts to the touch, knowing that it is by a woman, and it is this woman who comes forth to be identified in fear and trembling, telling him the whole truth. Jesus recognizes the claims her faith has made on him, and the part her faith has played in her healing. He calls her "Daughter" and in some way is empowered by her actions to take charge of events. Jesus takes control of the second healing by disregarding the premature announcements of the child's death, ignoring the laughter, and ejecting weepers and mourners. He takes witnesses he has chosen, the child's parents and selected disciples, into the room where the girl lies, and grasps her hand, saying to her, "Little girl, I say to you, Arise!" It is Jesus' recognition of the grown woman's claim upon him that causes him to identify her as kin. She has brought forth in him power to realize God's healing realm, and is now daughter among brothers, sisters, and mothers who do the will of God.

When Jesus returns to Nazareth in chapter 6, he is identified as a carpenter, the son of Mary (or as son of a carpenter and of

Mary) and brother of James, Joses, Judas, Simon, and their sisters. Already we know that familial identity has been superseded, and so we are in a position to understand Jesus' ironic quip, "A prophet is not without honor except in his hometown, and among his own kin, and in his own house [*oikia*]," in a way the people of Nazareth cannot.

This familiar saying with its triple pattern of leaving household, kin, and home village or town also occurs elsewhere. The triple pattern itself is ancient: God commands Abraham to leave land, kinship group, and his father's house in Genesis 12:1. Whether in the first century or the age of the patriarchs, the household belongs in a structure that includes a kinship group identified within the wider community, be it village or town, of which it is a part. Jesus' saying implies that Nazareth speaks with a unified voice, with univocal expectations. Perhaps the context of the episode in Mark 6 implies that Nazareth might be unwilling or unable to recognize nonfamilial configurations of those who do God's will. It is this episode in Mark 6 that enables us to understand Jesus' implied departure in Mark's Gospel from Nazareth, his hometown, to ministry in and around Capernaum with Jesus moving, as his disciples did, from house to house.

Thus Mark's Gospel both implies and describes Jesus' departure from Nazareth to an area in and around Capernaum, characterizing Jesus and his disciples as law-abiding Jews who keep the commandments. Furthermore, the notion of a break between Jesus and his family of origin serves to identify a new family of followers, those who do the will of God. What has happened to Jesus' biological family?

For this kind of investigation, Mark 6 also provides a starting point. Jesus' brothers are James, Joses (or Joseph), Judas (or Jude), and Simon. Later Christian tradition calls Jesus' sisters Mary (or Mariam) and Salome, the two most common names for women in the first century CE. References to Jesus' brothers can be found in the writings of Hegesippus, which were preserved by the third-to-fourth-century church historian Eusebius.

Hegesippus reports that Jesus' father Joseph had a brother named Clopas. If this is the same Clopas whose wife Mary is identified at John 19:25 as standing by the cross, then Jesus' aunt Mary as well as his mother Mary witnessed his death.

In his letter to the Galatians Paul reports that he went to Jerusalem and visited "James, the Lord's brother" (1:19), a leader in the Jerusalem community. At a council in Jerusalem described in Acts 15, James also seems to be prominent, and the historian Josephus reports James's martyrdom by stoning in 62 CE at the instigation of the high priest Ananias. After James's martyrdom, Simeon, the son of Clopas and Mary, succeeded his cousin as a leader in the Jerusalem community. He was martyred during the reign of Trajan (98–117 CE). As for Jesus' other brothers, Paul cites them as examples of traveling missionaries with their wives in 1 Corinthians 9:5; perhaps he is referring to Joses, Judas, and Simon. Finally, a local martyr called Conon, whose name was attached to a cave beneath the Church of the Annunciation in Nazareth, was said to have died during the persecution of Christians under the Emperor Decius in 250–51 CE. According to the account of his martyrdom, Conon was employed as a gardener on the imperial estate at Magydos in Pamphylia, Asia Minor (modern Turkey). When questioned about his place of origin and ancestry, he replied, "I am of the city of Nazareth in Galilee; I am of the family of Christ, whose worship I have inherited from my ancestors." This link to Jesus' hometown of Nazareth may be the last ancient reference to Jesus' family's descendents. Perhaps this suggests that Jesus' family from Nazareth in subsequent generations reversed the rejection Jesus experienced during his lifetime.

Disciples in the synoptic Gospels, like Jesus, are good Jews who keep the commandments to honor father and mother. Discipleship, however, first of all means following Jesus and separating from families, houses, possessions, and professions (such as fishing) for a ministry of preaching from house to house in an urban setting, presuming the cultural norm of hospitality. Unlike Jesus, who never returned to his family of origin, his disciples may return (as Jesus had implied) to families, houses, and professions — but not to their fathers.

Matthew and Luke focus on Jesus' family of origin; Mark and John do not. Matthew's description of the flight of the Holy Family into Egypt and their return to Nazareth demonstrates the upright, law-abiding character of Joseph, who heeds the word of God and thereby fulfills Hebrew prophecy and saves the life of "the child and his mother." Luke's portrait of the miraculous parallel births of John the Baptist to Elizabeth and Jesus to Mary places Jesus within an extended family whose priestly pedigree he shares. His moral and spiritual growth witness to God's favor; his fidelity to God is set over and against honoring his parents, yet Luke describes his obedience to them.

Mark's Gospel, on the other hand, assumes a Nazareth connection and does identify Jesus' mother, brothers, and sisters, even though the focus is on the rift between Jesus and his family of origin and hometown. Jesus' true father is God. John's Gospel presumes this family division as well, and fails entirely to mention Joseph. Through his heavenly origins and his own words, Jesus remains apart from any maternal claims: he addresses Mary as "Woman," not "Mother." Through his dying words from the cross, however, Jesus brings a new family into being. He hands this "woman" over to the beloved disciple and invites him to call her "Mother."

Chapter Three

MATTHEW'S
NEW FAMILY

WE ALL KNOW that there are four Gospels within the canon of scripture, but do we really pay attention to what that means? How often, when "the Gospel" is read in church, do we listen to it with an awareness that this is the one "according to *Matthew*" or "according to *John*"? It may be easy to recognize John, but how many of us could tell, just from listening to a short passage, whether it was from Matthew, Mark, or Luke?

Many people approach the New Testament thinking that the four Gospels basically say the same thing, just in slightly different ways. Many think that there is one gospel narrative with different bits of it contributed by the different Gospels. Such thinking reflects a long history of attempts, many by illustrious scholars, to *harmonize* the four Gospels, to make them all agree with each other. One of the earliest was a second-century convert from Assyria named Tatian, who lived long before the canon of scripture, as we know it, was fixed. Tatian was trained in Greek philosophy, so we know he had a sophisticated education, and he wrote a popular work called the Diatessaron, *through/according to the four*, which was an attempt to put all the known stories about Jesus from four gospels into one continuous, coherent narrative. It is far easier to have one sequential story with no discrepancies or inconsistencies. We see how this works most obviously when we look at Christmas pageants. They omit any conflicts between

Matthew and Luke, and organize the story in such a way that the maximum number of elements can be included. This of course creates parts for the maximum number of children! The Christmas pageant, or crèche, is a modern text of its own; but it is not the text of any one of the Gospels. Sequential and consistent narrative is easier to live with, and to live by.

But the actions of the bishops, and the fourth-century councils which identified the canon of the New Testament as we know it, indicate that they believed it was important to preserve the four separate and different witnesses, tensions and difficulties notwithstanding. This is the pattern, after all, that is established in the Hebrew scriptures, with their two different stories in Genesis of the world's origin and separate sources for the history of Israel. The witness of scripture is not unitary; it is diverse and often self-contradictory, and within the books of scripture themselves there are interpretations of scripture. Paul, for example, interprets the Genesis story of Abraham and Sarah and Hagar in Galatians. Jesus interprets scripture every time he says, "You have heard it said . . . but I say. . . . " We believe that the scriptures were written by humans who were themselves inspired by the Holy Spirit. But if the scriptures contain multiple and self-contradictory witnesses, how are we to appropriate their message for ourselves?

This difficulty arises when we require our scriptures to have unequivocal answers to our questions, as do many who consider themselves Christians today. But if we ask ourselves, "How would Jesus or Paul have read this scripture?" we may find a very different and interesting interpretational strategy. Jesus and Paul both lived and taught within the Jewish interpretive world of the first century. There were many forms of Judaism then, as there are now; one of dominant forms arose out of the school of the Pharisees, which became what we know as Rabbinic Judaism. We find Jesus being called "Rabbi," which means teacher, regularly in the Gospels, and Paul describes himself has having been trained by the Pharisee Gamaliel (Acts 22:3). Gamaliel is one of the rabbis cited in a collection of teachings called the Mishnah, addressing how the Jew should observe the Torah, the first five books of the Bible. Part of the authoritative tradition of interpretation within Judaism, the Mishnah gives us a window into how Jesus and Paul might have understood some ways in which scripture should be appropriated for living.

The first teaching of the Mishnah asks the question "From what time in the evening may one recite the Shema?" The Shema, which begins with Deuteronomy 6:4–9, is the prayer required by the Law to be recited twice a day, in the evening and in the morning, and is the foundational expression of the Jew's relationship with God. Now, it may not seem very important to us to get the time of a required prayer right; we have the sun and a clock to tell morning from evening. But that's not really what this question is about. The Mishnah responds by citing the rulings of several rabbinic authorities — but never provides a definitive answer. The answers to the second question, "Until when may one recite the evening Shema?" are illustrative. One rabbi says, "Until you can tell the difference between blue and black." Another says, "Until you can distinguish the features of a friend at a distance." What the Mishnah provides is not a compendium of answers to questions, but of strategies by which to address the questions. The point of the discussion is not so much to arrive at some answer; the point is to commit to struggling with the questions posed by scripture. Hearing and obeying God in scripture does not mean finding the answers, but struggling with the questions that scripture raises. Four different witnesses to the gospel present us with the need to struggle with our questions, to propose answers, and then to live according to the fruits of that struggle, trusting in the Spirit of God to guide our struggle and direct our ways.

Here we are wrestling with the different understandings of family construction and commitment to family presented in the New Testament. We have seen in the past two chapters that each of the four Gospels has a different narrative about Jesus' origins. Similarly, each Gospel has a different understanding of how Jesus interacted with his family of origin and construed the community of believers as family. Each Gospel arose within a different community and spoke to different needs, and thus reflected different understandings about inclusion and exclusion, authority and responsibility.

Jesus' Brothers and Sisters

Of all the Gospel communities, Matthew is the one most clearly situated in the context of Jewish rabbinic tradition. Matthew's presentation shows Jesus as concerned about observing Jewish Law, skilled in studying and debating that Law with others, and willing to be informed by others' arguments. Many scholars describe Matthew's community as a scribal community, and it is likely that the imprecations of Matthew 23 ("Woe to you, scribes and Pharisees...") are addressed as much to members of his own community as to external authorities. Jesus' teachings are collected into five discrete sections of Matthew's Gospel, which some scholars see as a representation of the five books of the Torah. Jesus delivers the opening collection of sayings which we know as the Sermon on the Mount while sitting on a mountain, evoking Moses' descent from the mountain with the Commandments. Matthew's Jesus expands upon the written laws of Torah with oral teaching in exactly the same fashion that the rabbinic teachings do. "You have heard it said, 'Do not commit adultery.' But I say, 'Do not look upon a woman with lust...'" (5:27).

Throughout the Gospel Matthew also shows Jesus responding to the challenge of incorporating non-Jewish believers into Matthew's deeply Jewish community. While there were provisions for converting to Judaism, at heart being Jewish was about being descended from the ancestral fathers, Abraham, Isaac, and Jacob. The "house of Israel" is not a metaphor; Israel was the other name of Jacob, and the house of Israel means the descendents of Jacob. The extent to which family controls participation in the Jewish community becomes apparent when one looks at inheritance law:

strictly speaking, there was no possibility of making a will under Jewish Law, because Torah determined succession absolutely. The observant Jew could not will his estate to someone outside the family, nor could he or she inherit from someone who was not a Jew. This made converting to Judaism problematic for very practical reasons, since the convert became ineligible to inherit from anyone.

Because inclusion in the Jewish community is so much a family matter, part of Matthew's task is to reframe family so that descent from Jacob or from Abraham is not required for full participation in the Matthean Jewish community. Matthew reserves the authority of "the fathers" to "the Father in heaven" alone. Only in the Gospel of Matthew does Jesus command his disciples, "Call no man father." In obedience to that command, Matthew's Gospel goes to considerable lengths to conceptualize its community as a family of those who do the will of Jesus' Father, who thereby become Jesus' brothers and sisters and mothers. Since God is the only Father Jesus recognizes, an absolute and uncompromising rejection of the role or authority of the human, biological father distinguishes the composition of this family.

As we saw in his treatment of the Holy Family, Matthew displaces the human father — Joseph, the husband of Jesus' mother, Mary, is never referred to as Jesus' father. Ancient Jewish genealogy followed a highly stylized form, a chain of "begats" wherein a father is identified as begetting one or more sons, with only those offspring that pertain to the succession being named. Matthew's genealogy contains three unusual features: female names, mention of unnamed "brothers," and an abrupt break in the pattern at the end. Female names are rarely included in a genealogy, and much ink has been used up trying to explain why four ancestral mothers are mentioned in Matthew's genealogy. One frequently proposed explanation identifies the four as coming from outside the Jewish lineage and nonetheless contributing to the house of Israel. Although Matthew's genealogy of Jesus establishes Joseph's patrilineal ancestry through a chain of "x begat y" relationships, that chain breaks after it reaches Joseph. There is no statement that "Joseph begat Jesus" or any other identification of Joseph as the father of Jesus; Matthew identifies Joseph only as the husband of Mary "of whom Jesus was born." Luke, on the other hand, has no problem calling Joseph Jesus' father (Luke 2:33, 48).

Elsewhere in Matthew, only two individuals are explicitly identified as fathers: Zebedee, father of James and John, whom they abandon in order to follow Jesus, and Herod, who is clearly not an exemplar of paternal virtues. Where the same basic episode appears in more than one Gospel, if there is mention of a father in it, Matthew will describe the person as a man, not a father. For example, the healing of the epileptic child appears in Matthew, Mark, and Luke, with varying details and different morals to the story, but where Mark and Luke easily label the child's father as "father," Matthew calls him only *anthropos,* human (17:14–21; Mark 9:14–29, Luke 9:37–43). Similarly, where Luke reports Jesus' saying, "What father among you, if his son asks for a fish, will instead give him a serpent?" Matthew rejects the word "father" and says instead *anthropos,* human; in both sources, the analogy is to the goodness of the heavenly Father, but Matthew will not even concede that there is an earthly one (7:9–10; Luke 11:11–12).

Matthew never reports Jesus as identifying any human being as "father." For Matthew's Jesus, the only worthy object of the label "father" is the Father in heaven. Nor does Jesus use the word "father" in a positive way to describe ancestors — instead, he condemns the scribes and Pharisees as being the "offspring of vipers," their ancestral fathers who murdered the prophets.

In one episode, Jesus rejects the human father in a way that is difficult even for us to accept, while the observant Jew then (and now) would find it completely unacceptable. A would-be disciple asks to bury his father before following Jesus. It is easier for us to accept Jesus' response, "Leave the dead to bury their dead," if we understand that Jesus was not telling the young man to leave a dead body without burying it, but rather to come now, and not wait for his father to die. Few modern adults would expect to put their vocations on hold until their parents have died, nor would their parents expect it. However, for the observant adult Jew of Jesus' time, the obligation to support one's aging parents was absolute. Perhaps Jesus' response to the aspiring disciple implies that a responsible human father will support the son's transference of allegiance from himself to the Father in heaven, and the human father who does not is already "dead." In the Matthean community, the abandonment of biological family does not stand in contradiction to the command to honor one's father and mother, if it is clearly understood that the disciple's father is God, and only God.

One way of identifying a person as father is to identify his son; thus when you say, "There goes Morty, Reuben's son," you are identifying Reuben as the father of Morty. Matthew's use of this shows whether people are members of the community in good standing, or excluded from the community; if you are behaving as the son of a human father, you can't be the son of the heavenly Father or a brother of Jesus. For example, after James and John leave Zebedee to follow Jesus they are occasionally described as the sons of Zebedee — but only when their (or their mother's) behavior excludes them from the family of Jesus, those who seek the will of God and do it. So we see their mother, described as "the mother of the sons of Zebedee," ask Jesus to seat them next to him in the kingdom of heaven (20:20). (Mark's Gospel has the same story, but there James and John are referred to by their names.) After Jesus has rebuked "the sons of Zebedee" and restored them to fellowship in Matthew, they are again described as "brothers." Similarly, in Gethsemane, where they fail Jesus by falling asleep, Matthew calls them "the sons of Zebedee," whereas Mark again refers to them as James and John. At the foot of the cross the "mother of the sons of Zebedee" is present; the sons themselves are conspicuous by their absence; they have again excluded themselves from the family for this event.

On the other hand, Matthew explicitly identifies James and John as brothers whenever they are behaving as brothers, specifically as brothers of Jesus, by doing the will of God. So when Jesus

sees "James the son of Zebedee and his brother John" with their
father in the boat, he calls them to follow him, and they respond
to that call by leaving the boat and leaving their father (4:21).
The phrase "the son of Zebedee" here functions as a surname,
identifying this particular James, rather than the other disciple
also named James who is the son of Alphaeus; it is like saying James Zebedee-son and James Alphaeus-son. When Peter and
James and John witness the Transfiguration of Jesus in a moment
of special revelation on the mountain, Matthew (unlike Mark and
Luke) again emphasizes the fraternal relationship, "James and his
brother John." So Matthew's Gospel is particularly intentional
about the use of language of sonship and brotherhood, in a context where only God may be called Father, and brothers of Jesus
are those who do the will of God.

Only in this Gospel, furthermore, does Jesus instruct the disciples to pray to God as "Our Father, the one in heaven." If you
use the King James Version of the Bible you will find this also in
Luke, but modern scholarship has discovered more reliable manuscripts than those which the KJV used, and modern translations
reflect the better manuscripts of Luke, rendering Luke's version
of the Lord's Prayer simply "Father, hallowed be your name."
Matthew's version serves to emphasize both the community nature of the prayer, and the correct location of the community's
Father — in heaven.

Most of the time when the word "father" appears in Matthew,
it is used by Jesus to refer to God — Jesus calls God "my Father,"
or, speaking to the disciples, "your Father." Yet Jesus does not use
this term indiscriminately, but only in the presence of the community that does the will of the Father, the community of sisters
and brothers and mothers of Jesus. Matthew's Jesus never calls
God "Father" when speaking to his adversaries or in the presence
of his critics, the scribes and Pharisees. In Matthew, therefore,
filial language toward God is reserved for use only among those
who constitute Jesus' true family, as Jesus understands it. Moreover, Matthew's use of the word "Father" for God significantly

outnumbers that of Mark or Luke, and about half the uses in Matthew identify God as Father to the disciples, "your/our Father," by contrast to the Gospel of John where God is called "your Father" only once, after the resurrection (before the resurrection in John, God is Father only to Jesus, "my Father").

So as Matthew understands it, the community of Jesus' followers constitutes a new family based not on biology but on behavior. Those who associate themselves with Jesus by doing the will of the heavenly Father become the brothers and sisters and mothers of Jesus, and offspring of the Father in heaven, and are therefore related *to each other* as brothers and sisters. There is no role for the human father in this community; the male who begets has equal standing with his offspring as a brother of Jesus and a child of the heavenly Father. The authority of the heavenly Father overrides any obligations of biological kinship and is mediated by the community as a whole.

This notion of family has significant implications for inheritance and property. As in any Jewish family, the offspring of the Father, not just those who intentionally do the will of the Father but also those who unknowingly do the Father's will by ministering to the brothers and sisters of Jesus, will inherit the Father's property, which is the kingdom of heaven. Today we expect to control the disposition of our estates after death by means of legal instruments such as wills and trusts. Jewish inheritance rules in Jesus' time, however, were strictly prescribed by Torah, and although some Jews adopted the Roman and Greek custom of making a will for bestowal of gifts on behalf of the deceased, they had no authority to designate heirs. To declare, as the king does in the discourse about the sheep and the goats in Matthew 25:31–46, that those "blessed by my Father" will "inherit the kingdom prepared for them" identifies them as the Father's heirs and *de facto* offspring, sons and daughters. These sons and daughters of the Father cannot be offspring of anyone else, since we can only have one Father, the one in heaven. In this discourse, those who inherit are persons of every nation or race (*ethne* in Greek, from which our word "ethnic" is derived), having in common only a history of compassionate behavior toward the least of Jesus' brothers and sisters, and thereby becoming themselves Jesus' brothers and sisters. In the Gospel of John 19, Jesus creates a family by fiat from those who gather around him; in Matthew 25, Jesus declares the whole world of compassionate souls to be one family, brothers and sisters of Jesus, heirs of the Father in heaven. The implications of Matthew's view of kinship and inheritance are astonishing, and a claim that Christian tradition has found difficult if not impossible to appropriate, but it is one Christians must recognize if we are to be honest about the Bible and family values.

Eunuchs in the Family

Matthew's claims about inheritance and inclusion in family lead to a novel understanding about the presence of eunuchs in families; the distance between our world and the world of Jesus is no more keenly felt than here, where we are compelled to face the profound otherness of Jesus' world. What can Jesus' teaching about eunuchs possibly say to us today? Why must we include a discussion of eunuchs when examining the implications for family values in Jesus' teachings?

We must include eunuchs in our discussion of family values because Matthew's Jesus raises the topic of eunuchs in the context of teaching on marriage. We cannot avoid eunuchs, but we can and must avoid reading our own understanding of the roles of eunuchs, informed by two millennia of church teaching on celibacy, into Jesus' teaching. Was Jesus primarily speaking of sexual abstinence when he declared that "some make themselves eunuchs for the sake of the kingdom," or did he have a different frame of reference? What is the relationship between Jesus' teaching about eunuchs in Matthew and the family as construed — brothers, sisters, and mothers with one heavenly Father — by the Matthean community?

Set within the context of Matthew 19, the passage is part of a larger whole focusing on instructions about marriage and kinship systems. A controversy begins with a question about divorce posed by the Pharisees, which leads to a discussion about the nature of marriage. Jesus' teaching, based on Genesis 2, prohibits divorce and forbids remarriage. The disciples, to a man, respond that if this is the case, then it would be better not to marry. Note that their unanimous dismay suggests a rather more liberal attitude to divorce than we might imagine. With intervening centuries of church-sponsored absolute prohibition on divorce, we forget that the realities of Jesus' world were not so far different from ours in this respect.

Jesus responds that indeed there is a "higher righteousness" not followed by all disciples but only by those who are able, namely, those who have made themselves eunuchs for the sake of the kingdom. Usually understood as an invitation to celibacy, Jesus' teaching on eunuchs is often taken to mean rejection of marriage altogether. In the very next sentence, however, Jesus admonishes disciples who prevent children from coming to him: "Let the little children come to me, and do not stop them; for it is to such as these that the kingdom of heaven belongs" (19:14). This is a forcible reminder that reading eunuchs as examples of celibacy makes little sense in the immediate context of the saying. If some make themselves eunuchs "for the sake of the kingdom" and if children are those to whom the kingdom belongs, what can we say about the relationship between eunuchs and families?

So what could Jesus have had in mind, and how would he have understood the value and role of eunuchs? Here we must look again at the Hebrew scriptures, writings of contemporaneous Jews like Philo of Alexandria, Josephus, and Luke, and writings of other Hellenistic authors of the period. Early Christian interpreters of the passage also help us to understand eunuchs from the perspective of the culture of the time. The very existence of a sizeable body of ancient literature addressing the roles and positions of eunuchs in the world of early Christianity makes it clear that eunuchs occupied a place of some significance in society. There is an important interpretive principle at work here: writers do not proscribe or prescribe behaviors for situations that do not exist. If, for example, we find writings that prohibit divorce, we can be fairly certain that divorce is fairly prevalent. If, on the other hand, authorities make a special effort to *commend* a particular activity, like childbearing and rearing, one should suspect that it has fallen into disfavor, as happened under Augustus, who had to legislate financial incentives for marrying and having children. We live in a world where we do not find it necessary to legislate against self-castration, but that is not the world Jesus lived in.

One *locus classicus* for eunuchs was in palaces and royal courts, where they often achieved high status and rank because of their single-minded devotion and trustworthiness. In the ancient courts of Israel and Judah, eunuchs served as *sarisim,* or civil functionaries. (Although the word *saris* [plural *sarisim*]) is usually translated by the English words denoting "officials" or "servants," standard biblical Hebrew lexica give "eunuch" as its meaning, and the ancient Greek translation of the Hebrew scriptures, the Septuagint, uses *eunouchos* for *saris.*) These were servants connected with the queen's quarters and were in service to the queen. They appear beginning possibly with the time of Jehu and Jezebel (2 Kings 9) and their presence continues to the fall of Judah and beyond. 1 Samuel 8:15 warns Israelites about the conduct of kings: "He will take the tenth of your grain and of your vineyards and give it to his eunuchs and to his servants," sometimes translated "officers and courtiers." At the fall of Jerusalem in 586 BCE, 2 Kings 24:12 identifies eunuchs accompanying King Jehoiachin into exile in Babylon with other members of his court, his mother, servants, and officials.

We encounter eunuchs in the New Testament outside Matthew. Acts 8 describes an Ethiopian eunuch in the court of the queen of the Ethiopians. The Ethiopian eunuch may be a proselyte or a Jew of the Diaspora. Nothing about the reported encounter of the eunuch with Philip suggests anything irregular or unusual. In fact, some manuscript traditions add Acts 8:37, recording a dialogue of the eunuch with Philip. Philip declares, "If you believe with all your heart, you may be baptized." The eunuch replies, "I believe that Jesus Christ is the Son of God." This declaration, made by an African high-ranking court official, may be the earliest confessional statement in Acts. The eunuch is baptized and departs rejoicing.

Scripture recognizes that eunuchs contributed positively to the political and spiritual history of Israel. The court eunuch Ebedmelech interceded with King Zedekiah on behalf of Jeremiah, rescuing the prophet from certain death in a cistern (Jer. 38:7). But eunuchs also present a problem for the Jewish community. The Torah refuses entry to the assembly of the Lord to someone with crushed testicles or whose penis is cut off. Part of the covenant is the injunction to "be fruitful and multiply," to have children, and the raising of children to walk in the way of the Lord is a primary obligation and a blessing. Eunuchs are not able to beget children, although one common function of eunuchs in Hellenistic society was the education and nurturing of children. Jewish moral tradition also condemned castration as an act offensive to nature, because of the loss of male potency and identity. The Jewish philosopher Philo is entirely condemnatory particularly because of what he sees to be eunuchs' transgression of categories of masculinity; he calls them "hybrids of man and woman." Josephus is equally disparaging, but he appointed a eunuch as a tutor to his own son and notes the presence of eunuchs in the court of Herod.

The actual presence of eunuchs in the Jewish community, moreover, mandated accommodation. Isaiah 56:1–7 is a prophecy of inclusion for all in the day of salvation, of which Matthew was sufficiently aware to quote in 21:13. In Isaiah 56:3–5, the Lord says that the eunuch who keeps Sabbath and observes the covenant will no longer consider himself a "dry tree," one without progeny and therefore without a future in the day of salvation, but will have an everlasting name within the Lord's house and walls "which will not be cut off." In this prophecy, both eunuchs and "strangers" or "foreigners," i.e., non-Jews, who join themselves to Israel through observing the judgments of the Lord, doing justice, keeping the Sabbath, and refraining from unrighteousness, are promised participation in Israel's worship of the Lord. Thus Isaiah prophecies a community in which membership will be determined neither by ancestry (fathers), nor by ability to have children, but rather by active observance of the commandments and participation in the covenant. Echoing this, Wisdom 3:13–14 associates faithful eunuchs with barren women; both will receive blessing from the Lord.

Some early Christians read Matthew's teaching on making oneself a eunuch for the sake of the kingdom literally. The earliest report of the desire for castration among Christians comes from the second-century Justin Martyr. In his *Apology* 1:29 he defends Christians against accusations that they practiced promiscuous intercourse by describing the extent of their desire for purity. Justin explains that one of "our number" recently presented to Felix, the prefect in Alexandria, a petition, "asking that permission might be given to a doctors to make him a eunuch; for the doctor said that they were forbidden to do this without the permission of the prefect." When the procurator refused, the youth remained single, and, Justin continues, was satisfied with the testimony of his own conscience and that of his fellow believers. Another third-century Christian writer, Origen of Alexandria, castrated himself in an early excess of enthusiasm, but later denounced a literal reading of Matthew 19:12. Instead he reframed the understanding of self-eunuchization and denounced castration as the morally weaker choice: a "true" eunuch is not one who eliminates the ability to have sex, but one who eliminates the desire for sex.

His predecessor, Bishop Melito of Sardis, was known as a eunuch, but this was probably a reference to his celibacy and not to self-castration, for which there is no evidence. Melito thus stood in the tradition of eunuchs who were ideal servants, bodyguards, and managers because they are cut off from normal family life. They are brave because they have nobody they love more than their master and, because they are objects of contempt, they have an even greater loyalty to their master. In a sense they are like the children of the family, although without biological family ties — their master is their family. This is the role which Melito plays in his church, which is not his own but God's. Further, Melito is estranged from his Jewish family and cut off from networks of relationships and support accessible to others. His celibacy is the means to perfect service of God.

However we interpret Jesus' saying about "eunuchs for the kingdom of heaven," clearly it has significant implications for family in Matthew's Gospel. The saying stands as an intensification of the demands of discipleship and presents an alternative to marriage. Jesus commends eunuchizing oneself for the sake of the kingdom, although only some will accept and act upon this saying. Here the Greek verb is used reflexively, with a personal pronoun, to describe voluntary action undertaken upon oneself, for the sake of the kingdom of heaven. An analogous use of a verb describing voluntary action for the sake of the kingdom is *tapeinoō*, meaning "to humble or abase." Matthew 18:4 describes an individual who *humbles himself* like this child as greatest in the kingdom of heaven. The voluntary nature of such humility is clear from other passages in which Jesus declares that whoever *exalts himself* will be humbled, and whoever *humbles himself* will be exalted. To humble oneself, according to Jesus, is similar to becoming like a little child — lowering one's status voluntarily to that of a child. The same is true of those who have eunuchized themselves, voluntarily making themselves dependent on God within a community of dependents.

Eunuchs in the Matthean community, having voluntarily given up all honor deriving from family, possessions, and wealth, are exclusively loyal to the kingdom. All hope of honor and status is now derived from the heavenly Father. Moreover, whatever status is acquired through proximity and service to the heavenly

Father cannot be passed to one's heirs. To Peter's poignant question posed after Jesus' teaching about eunuchs, "Look, we have left everything and followed you. What then will we have?" Jesus offers status and power not in this world, but in the next. Jesus promises Peter that when the Son of Man is seated on the throne of his glory, those followers will also sit on twelve thrones, "judging the twelve tribes of Israel. And every one who has left houses or brothers or sisters or father or mother or children or lands, for my name's sake, will receive a hundredfold, and will inherit eternal life" (19:27–29). If some of Matthew's disciples are taking Jesus' injunctions seriously enough to make themselves the equivalent of children or slaves, they have no heirs or possessions in this life.

It is extraordinary to note how few current studies on Jesus and the family take this saying about eunuchs seriously or accord it an extended discussion. If Matthew 19:12 is mentioned at all, it is usually in a category shaped by modern understanding, such as an injunction to singleness within the overall category of marriage. Thus singleness would be regarded as a transitional state before or between marriages, or the passage might be understood to commend a vocation to celibacy. On the contrary, Jesus is not talking about single people, be they unmarried or widowed, or people with celibate vocations. There are many other ways to commend sexual continence: for example, Paul boasts of his unmarried state, and praises the single person and the widowed without ever mentioning eunuchs. To ignore ancient understandings of eunuchs in Israelite, Persian, Hellenistic Greek, Nubian, Byzantine, and Chinese history is to impoverish our understanding of the text.

To recognize eunuchs as full members of the Matthean community, however, casts new light upon roles and titles. On the basis of this saying, some have argued that Matthew's community is an ascetic or celibate community. We have seen from the teachings on children and from the inclusion of mothers in the community that this is unlikely. But the presence of voluntary (and involuntary) eunuchs in the community seems certain. The injunction of Matthew 23:9, to call no man father on earth, "for you have one Father, who is in heaven," is often understood to describe Matthew's community as one of equals under one heavenly Father. Those who obey the command to "call no man father" must also surrender their own right to be called father with all the privilege attendant upon that right. They must surrender also their claim on their offspring, who become children of the one Father in heaven. The begetter's responsibility for care and nurturing of the children remains as part of his responsibility toward the whole community, but he has become, effectively, Isaiah's "dry tree," a eunuch. Here is another way that some "make themselves eunuchs" for the sake of the kingdom. In a community where some cannot beget, one way to ensure equality may be to require that all surrender the privilege of fatherhood.

Jesus' teaching on eunuchs poses a particular challenge to those who regard "family values" as synonymous with heterosexual marriage, since Jesus' commendation of those who become eunuchs specifically *undermines* male heterosexual privilege. At the heart of Jesus' message commending certain social behaviors for men and women lies a refusal to claim the privilege and power of the father, which belong only to God. In contemporary discussions of sexual identity, Matthew 19 reminds us that Jesus commends to some of his disciples the absolute severing of family ties and complete subordination for the sake of the kingdom.

Insiders and Outsiders

In this chapter we have explored the roles of children and eunuchs in Matthew's Gospel, but what about another vulnerable group — the outsiders, or Gentiles, in Matthew's primarily Jewish community? Jesus apparently undergoes a significant change of heart regarding Gentiles during the course of the narrative. Twice Jesus indicates that his mission is only to Jews — in other words, his vision is narrow. In 10:5–6, he sends out the disciples with the instruction not to go among the Gentiles, but only to the "lost sheep of the house of Israel," and in 15:24 he says he was sent only to the "lost sheep of the house of Israel." But there are several instances in Matthew where Gentiles and kinship language intersect and where Jesus confounds our expectations by going to those beyond the "lost sheep of the house of Israel." How do Gentiles fare in Matthew's community?

First, it is important to remember that Jewish Torah pays significant attention to the issue of foreigners (Gentiles) and sojourners living among the people of Israel. Special provisions are made for them because God loves the stranger and Israel's defining memory is that of being strangers in the land of Egypt (Deut. 10:18–19, Exod. 22:21, 23:9). Strangers must be permitted to rest on the Sabbath, there must be one justice for stranger and Israelite alike, and strangers, often rendered "aliens" in modern translations, are not to be oppressed. Note that what defines a stranger is lack of descent from the ancestors of Israel; the stranger is one from outside the house of Israel. So these provisions for strangers demonstrate, in essence, concern for those who are outside the family, for those who do not come from Israelite, or Jewish, fathers. But no stranger may eat the Passover meal without being circumcised.

Later, in Isaiah 56, however, the stranger who observes the Sabbath does the Lord's pleasure, keeps the covenant, and enjoys the same welcome into the heavenly mountain and festive celebration as the eunuch discussed above. The Lord's house "shall be called a house of prayer for all nations" (56:7), and the prayers and offerings of the observant stranger will be accepted there. The prophetic witness expands the Torah's concern for the stranger into a positive welcome. Similarly, Matthew's Jesus found he had to expand the range of his mission.

Matthew's Gospel includes two stories of Jesus healing Gentiles in a family context. In Matthew 8:5–14, a centurion comes to Jesus seeking healing for his *pais*. Now *pais* is a Greek word whose first two lexical definitions are "child," referring to status as offspring, or "youth," referring to age. Only the third definition implies a condition of servitude, a slave or servant, but "servant" is the term used in most modern translations. This translation loses the kinship and childhood connotations of the word, which suggest that the centurion's *pais* is certainly a boy, and could be the centurion's own son. Furthermore, Jesus commends the faith of the centurion in terms that place the situation squarely into a context of family: "Truly I say to you, I have not found such faith in anyone *in Israel*." He goes on to say that it will be the foreigners, "many from east and west," who will eat with the ancestral fathers Abraham, Isaac, and Jacob in the kingdom of heaven, to the exclusion of the heirs. Thus the foreign centurion's concern for a child in his household, perhaps his own child, together with his unequivocal faith in Jesus, leads Jesus to reframe the house of Israel to include some not born into it, and to exclude some who claim to be heirs.

A second Gentile healing appears in Matthew 15:21–28, the story of the Canaanite woman, which takes place on the geographical borders of Israel. A foreign woman loudly seeks healing for her daughter and is rebuffed by the disciples and Jesus: "I was not sent except to the lost sheep of the house of Israel." But she persists in her plea, kneeling in front of him. He says, "It is not right to give the children's food to the dogs." She rejoins, "Yes, Lord, but even the dogs eat the crumbs that fall from their master's table." At this, Jesus commends the woman's faith, and heals the daughter (again, like the centurion, at a distance and without physical contact). Here again the healing concerns a child, and in this case explicitly a mother and daughter. Jesus at first excludes the woman from participation in his family, but she does not presume to claim family membership, she asks only the privilege granted to the basest of creatures in the household. By healing her daughter, Jesus raises them both to the status of children eating at the table. The context of this story supports this reading; immediately following this story is the teaching and healing of probably non-Jewish crowds who praise "the God of Israel," on the Gentile side of the Sea of Galilee. Just as Jesus has "fed" the

Canaanite woman with healing, he now feeds the seven thousand Gentiles with bread and fish.

Both the centurion and the Canaanite woman give Jesus a reason to rethink his mission and extend it beyond the house of Israel.

Beginnings and endings are places where the audience is expected to pay particular attention, and Gentiles figure significantly in several such places in Matthew. In the genealogy, Matthew evokes the memory of Gentile origins with the inclusion of Tamar and Rahab, who were Canaanites, Ruth, who was a Moabite, and "the wife of Uriah the Hittite," Bathsheba, possibly a Gentile herself. Magi worship at the house in Bethlehem and avoid disclosing its location to Herod. At the end of all Jesus' public teaching, his final discourse is the story of the sheep and the goats (Matt. 25:31–46), which is about the final judgment of *all the nations,* Gentiles and Jews. Those who inherit the kingdom, who become by fiat the heirs and therefore the offspring of the Father in heaven, qualify by reason of their compassionate behavior to the least of the brothers of the Son of Man. They have fed the hungry, given drink to the thirsty, received the stranger, clothed the naked, cared for the sick, visited the prisoner. Those who have ministered to the lowest and most abased of humanity are those who, in the end, become full members of the family of the Father, and heirs of his kingdom. There is no distinction between Jew and Gentile, only between those who behaved with compassion and those who did not. This discourse belongs to Matthew's Gospel alone as the conclusion of Jesus' public ministry, so it is crucial for an understanding of Matthew's community values.

At the very end of the Gospel, in another passage unique to Matthew, Jesus tells his disciples to "make disciples of *all the nations,* baptizing them into the name of the Father and the Son and the Holy Spirit." This inclusion of Gentiles, like the inclusion of eunuchs, demonstrates the absence of genealogical requirements for full membership in the family of Jesus. The stranger is brought near, into full filial relationship with the one Father in heaven, and becomes a bona fide brother or sister of Jesus, eligible for all the perquisites of family.

Women in Matthew's Family

The same Gentile women who appear so early in Matthew's Gospel — Tamar, Rahab, Ruth, and Bathsheba — all contribute significantly to our understanding of the place of women in Matthew's new family, where no man may claim the right to fatherhood. There is no prohibition against calling women "mother," however, and human mothers, unlike fathers, are retained in the family that Jesus reconstitutes with the words, "Whoever does the will of my Father in heaven is my brother and sister and mother." We have become accustomed to seeing the standard Greek usage of the male form *adelphoi* as a collective term to include brothers and sisters, but here "sisters" are explicitly included by using the feminine plural form of the word in addition to the male. So in this new family of those who do the Father's will, there are two named roles for women, *mother* and *sister*, but only one for men, *brother*. Perhaps the role of sister, defined by fraternal relationship rather than by status as child-bearer, provides a female counterpart to the male eunuch. On the other hand, in the ancient world wives were often referred to as "sister," as in the Song of Songs and 1 Corinthians 9:5. This in no way implies incest; what it indicates is greater permanence in the relationship than might be found in marriage, in a world where divorce was prevalent. Those who know his family in Nazareth identify Jesus' sisters as present and living in the community. Since sisters are explicitly named among those whom disciples leave behind (19:29), we may assume that Jesus, like the disciples, left his sisters in Nazareth for the sake of the kingdom.

Matthew uses the word "mother" rarely to identify specific women. Jesus' mother, Mary, of course, accounts for the majority of uses, mostly in the birth narrative and in the episode where she and Jesus' brothers come to see him while he is preaching, giving rise to the saying "Who are my mother and brothers? . . . .whoever does the will of my Father." Two mothers also appear at the foot of the cross. Tamar, Rahab, Ruth, and Bathsheba, although they are not specifically called "mothers," appear in a context to which their motherhood is integral. In fact, each of these women is assertive either in achieving motherhood or in securing her off-spring's future: Tamar risks her life, and Ruth her reputation, to become pregnant and so fulfill their sacred obligation to raise up children to deceased first husbands. Rahab recognizes that, through Joshua, the Lord will ultimately triumph, and she be-comes a traitor to her home city Jericho in order to secure a future for her family. Bathsheba collaborates with the prophet Nathan to secure the succession for Solomon her son, and so participates in bringing about the will of the Lord. All four women are bold, resourceful, and intrepid in furthering their families' existence and well-being in accord with the will of God. The actions of Tamar, Ruth, and Bathsheba also serve to identify them as authoritative figures within their families, where they rectify the behavior of the flawed or absent men who failed to take action to fulfill the will of the Lord.

The Canaanite woman who seeks healing for her child is similarly bold, resourceful, and authoritative in challenging and ultimately changing Jesus' attitude for the sake of her daughter. The mother of the sons of Zebedee, misguided though she may have been in asking for the positions of greatest honor for her sons, exhibits the same characteristics. Furthermore, Jesus does not hold her responsible for misunderstanding the will of the Father, since he addresses his rebuke to the sons who put her up to it.

In Matthew's narrative, mothers are a force to be reckoned with and an indispensable component of the family of Jesus. They overcome all obstacles and undergo considerable risk to fulfill the will of God themselves, both by bearing children and by acting on their behalf. Furthermore, these women make men accountable when they are slow to fulfill the will of God.

There is another mother in Matthew, who is Jesus himself. In Matthew 9:20–22, a grown woman seeks healing from an infirmity that isolates her from family and may have rendered her infertile. Jesus heals her, and calls her "Daughter." But we know that Jesus cannot consider himself her father because there is only one Father, in heaven. So if Jesus is assuming a parental role, it must be as a mother. And it is precisely the role of mother that Jesus claims toward the end of Matthew's Gospel. As he finishes a series of woes against scribes and Pharisees at the end of Matthew 23, the language of righteous ire changes to lament. In deepest sorrow, and within the grounds of the Jerusalem Temple, Jesus grieves over the coming fate of the city that slaughters prophets sent to it by God. He predicts the fall of Jerusalem. He declares his ardent longing to protect her children: "How often have I desired to gather your children together as a hen gathers her brood under her wings, and you were not willing! See, your house is left to you, desolate" (23:37–38). Not all mothers are good mothers. Mother Jerusalem has betrayed her role, and Jesus volunteers to replace her as a good, protecting mother.

Other domestic animals play a role in Matthew's households. The magi must have arrived on camels, and dogs eat the crumbs under the table in the story of the Canaanite woman. Sheep and goats are separated in Matthew's description of the Last Judgment. So household and family values in Matthew's Gospel certainly extend to the care of some domestic animals, although goats were probably not allowed inside the house.

Matthew's Community and Family Values

We have four different Gospels in the New Testament, each with its own distinctive context and emphasis. Of the four, Matthew's reflects the community most clearly embedded in and committed to Torah-observant Judaism. Matthew's Jesus teaches as the rabbis did with the reiterated phrase "You have heard it said,"

but intensifies the Law with his added "but I say to you," placing a more stringent demand upon the adherent. Just as Jesus
"raises the bar" with regard to Torah commands, he also intensifies the demands of community life by styling his community
as a family of sisters, brothers, and mothers under one heavenly
Father who is the sole paternal authority over the community. In
Matthew 23:9, Jesus commands, "Call no man your father on
earth, for you have one Father, the one in heaven," and Matthew
is careful to use father language in a way consistent with that
demand. If no man is to be called father, then all must surrender paternal authority to the heavenly Father. Similarly, Matthew
23:8 states that none are to be called rabbi, for all are brothers
and sisters with only one teacher. Some modern translations use
the word "students" here for the Greek *adelphoi,* which means
specifically "brothers" or "brothers and sisters," and this unwarranted gloss obscures the explicitly familial language with which
Matthew shapes his community.

Forgiveness is the glue of Matthew's community, therefore of
family life. The Lord's Prayer establishes the principle of mutual
and communal forgiveness: as you (plural) forgive others their
trespasses, so the heavenly Father will forgive you. However, if
you do not forgive others, neither will the heavenly Father forgive you. The community that prays this corporate prayer to *Our*
Father must be a community characterized by mutual forgiveness.

How that forgiveness works out in community life is explored
in Matthew 18, which is entirely about community life. It contains
Jesus' teaching on humility, on not despising fellow believers or
"little ones" or causing them to stumble, on regulating the community through discipline administered by the community, and
on forgiveness, which is illustrated by the parable of the unforgiving servant. In this parable, a king calls a servant to account for
a massive sum of money that has been entrusted to his management. He cannot, and the king orders him and his whole family to
be sold to make restitution. The servant pleads for mercy, and the
king forgives the entire debt. The servant, however, immediately

calls in a tiny debt owed him by another servant, and refuses his plea for mercy, throwing him into prison. Their fellow servants report this to the king, and the king rescinds the remittance of the debt owed by the unforgiving servant, and delivers him to punishment.

The parable expands Jesus' teaching on forgiveness by emphasizing the compassion, pity, and mercy of the king for his irresponsible or dishonest servant and the community responsibility for its members. It is the community of fellow slaves who, upon seeing the unforgiving behavior of the unjust servant, report his behavior to the king. Without community intervention, the debtor imprisoned by the unjust slave would have languished and perhaps died in prison. The king would have known nothing of the unjust servant's behavior. The king assumes that his forgiving behavior is being extended by the forgiven slave to his fellow slaves, so the king's retribution is all the more severe when he discovers the unjust servant's harsh behavior. The conclusion is the response to Peter's hoping to limit forgiveness to "seven times." By telling his disciples that they are to forgive "not seven times but seventy-seven times," Jesus exhorts the community to be merciful without limit. Those who do not forgive a brother or sister will be excluded. The love of God motivates community members to compassion, emphasizing interior orientation and true sincerity. Since the community is the true family, forgiveness, compassion, love of God, justice, care of the younger and weaker members, all these community values are the family values of Matthew.

Since there are to be no human authority figures in the community, the community as a group of equal sisters, brothers, and mothers must collectively assume responsibility for the well-being of all who are in it, and adjudicate and administer discipline when required. Matthew 18 describes how the community should operate internally, with its prime directives being humility, concern for the weakest among the community, and unlimited forgiveness. Although Jesus gave authority to bind and loose to Peter in

Matthew 16:19, in 18:18 Jesus distributes precisely that same authority in precisely the same words to the community as a whole, but here introduced with the emphatic formula "Truly (*amen*) I say to you...." The community together in prayer will discern the authority which the heavenly Father exercises over his family. Matthew's rejection of individual human paternal privilege is absolute and uncompromising.

Matthew's community is not an ascetic community; marriage is permitted, and there are wives in the community. But here as elsewhere, Jesus "raises the bar" on teaching about divorce. When asked to comment on the Deuteronomic exception permitting divorce, Jesus rejects divorce except on grounds of adultery, citing the creation narrative of Genesis 2 as a higher authority than the later concessions of Moses' Law. He reads deviation from the goodness of creation as hardness of heart, with divorce as its consequence. If we understand that Matthew's Jesus considered divorce to be a consequence of alienation from creation, Jesus' commendation of humility in Matthew is part and parcel of reading creation as awareness of finite existence, of dependence on God, and recognizing the consequences of excessive human desire for control.

Jesus' extraordinary teaching about becoming eunuchs "for the sake of the kingdom" is embedded in Matthew's discussion of divorce. Voluntary eunuchs, having divested themselves of all interest in their own human family, become full members of the family of Christ under the sole fatherhood of God. Involuntary eunuchs, those cut off from family by accident or birth defect or by the act of another, slave-dealer or slave-owner or practitioner of another religion, are equally welcome as full participants in the Father's family. Children are under special protection, and become paradigms for those who want to enter the kingdom of heaven. Their dependence and powerlessness model the appropriate stance before the heavenly Father. Abuse of a child is among the most heinous of sins.

Membership in the family is secured not by biological lineage or marriage, but solely by doing the will of its Father in heaven: humbling oneself like a child or a eunuch, practicing unconditional forgiveness, showing compassion to the least of the Father's children. Thus secured, membership entitles one to full participation in the inheritance of the Father's family, namely, the kingdom of heaven.

Chapter Four

LUKE'S
RESPECTABLE FAMILY

FROM ITS OPENING PAGES, Luke's Gospel plunges readers into a world where an angel announces miraculous births to the elderly husband of a barren woman and to her relative, a young girl engaged to be married. Their children are the focus of the narrative. The births may be miraculous, but the families into which the children are born typify the respectable family of the Greek-speaking, Roman-dominated Jewish world of the time. By contrast with Matthew, there is no attempt here to distance Jesus from Joseph; in fact, Jesus is born in Bethlehem because he is embedded in Joseph's lineage. When Jesus is presented in the Temple, Luke refers to Joseph and Mary as "the child's father and mother" in 2:33. Luke has no program like Matthew's to reframe the family. In fact, in much of the material that is unique to Luke, the classical family itself is a primary context providing a bridge for Luke to his respectable and probably rather conservative audience; the "most excellent" Theophilus, to whom both the Gospel and Acts are addressed, would have been an educated patron or an investigating official. Nonetheless, Luke lays the ground for enlarging the function and role of family and household with a program of expanding hospitality. Disciples may need to leave their families of origin, and those families will need to extend themselves further in hospitality than might be considered usual.

The importance Luke attaches to the household as foundational shows up in a close comparative reading of one brief teaching of Jesus reported by both Matthew and Luke, the saying about the person who builds a house. In Matthew 7:24–27 Jesus says, "Therefore everyone who hears these words of mine and acts upon them will be like a wise man who built his house on rock. The rain fell, the floods came, and the winds blew and beat on that house, but it did not fall, because it had been founded on rock. And everyone who hears these words of mine and does not act on them will be like the foolish man who built his house on sand. The rain fell, and the floods came, and the winds blew and beat against that house, and it fell — and great was its fall!" There is no detail about the actual process of building here, and Matthew's visual image suggests a person setting up a house either on existing rock or on sand. Compare this with Luke 6:48–49: "That one is like a man building a house, who *dug deeply* and *laid the foundation* on rock; when a flood arose, the river burst against that house but could not shake it, because it had been well built. But the one who hears and does not act is like a man who built a house on the ground *without a foundation*. When the river burst against it, immediately it fell, and great was the ruin of that house." Luke emphasizes the householder's investment of effort in his house more than the choice of a building site. Luke's understanding of solid house construction is of an entirely different order from Matthew's; Luke describes the hard work of digging a foundation and compares that kind of builder with one who simply erects a house on the ground without digging a foundation. Luke's solid house is more expensive to build, and requires more resources. Further, Luke's phrasing suggests a connection between the downfall of the house and the downfall of the associated household. For Luke, the solidity of the house may directly correlate to the stability of the household.

Houses and households, and the families that create and inhabit them, are crucial to Luke's program to make Jesus credible to an educated and cultured audience. Jesus requires households to welcome those who cannot reciprocate, expanding an understanding of hospitality and providing family bases for the extension of the ministry. The communities formed by these households and their guest-members become the locus for enactment of unconditional forgiveness, and eventually replace the Temple as the locus for community worship.

Luke lays the foundation for the Gospel in its record of the births of John the Baptist and Jesus.

Birth Narrative

Luke's birth narrative begins by describing the situation with Zechariah and Elizabeth in phrases deliberately evoking the household of Abraham and Sarah, the foundational household of Israel. It's easy to miss the literary connections when reading the English, but the Greek that Luke uses echoes passages in the Septuagint, the Greek translation of Hebrew scriptures, where God opens and closes women's wombs. Luke writes, *"Now* it happened in the days of Herod . . . and there was no child . . . and both were *advanced in years."* Compare Genesis 18:11, *"Now* Abraham and Sarah were *advanced in age;* it had ceased to be with Sarah after the manner of women." The narratives, like the phrasing they are written in, parallel each other in important ways; two aged, childless wives of pious husbands conceive by the intervention of God. The announcements come through angels, meet with skepticism, and prove to be true. The household out of which Israel arose becomes the pattern for the extended household into which Jesus is born.

The Gospel's opening scene occurs in the Temple in Jerusalem, and this location itself plays an important role in Luke's history. The prophecy given to Zechariah as he burns incense includes not only the announcement of John's unlikely conception, but also a description of his future prophetic activity in unusual terms. The angel says that John will "turn the hearts of the fathers to the children, and the disobedient to the wisdom of the just; to make ready a people prepared for the Lord" (1:17 KJV). Despite, or perhaps because of, Luke's commitment to a deeply conventional concept of family life, he sees a need not for the exhortation of *children* to obey their *parents,* but for the hearts of *fathers* to be converted in favor of their *children.* The *paterfamilias* of the elite family in the Roman world, we recall, had absolute power over those of his household; the father in a Jewish household had similar power, only slightly modified by a need for community ratification of extreme disciplinary actions. The unexpected twist directing the hearts of the fathers to the children in this prophecy signals us to look carefully in the continuing work for unusual demands of discipleship.

Luke interweaves the birth narratives of John the Baptist and Jesus by attaching them to narratives about the relationship of their mothers, Elizabeth and Mary. The angel Gabriel announces Mary's pregnancy in the sixth month of Elizabeth's pregnancy. The first thing Mary does after learning of her pregnancy is to go to Elizabeth's home. She remains there three months, and then she returns to her own house. Mary's home has been the place of angelic visitation, and Elizabeth's home is the site of ecstatic utterance for both the pregnant Mary's song of praise (1:46–55) and later, for Zechariah's prophetic song over the newborn John (1:68–79).

By contrast with Matthew's infancy narrative, characterized by the contingency of Joseph's potential rejection of Mary, the terror of Herod's murderous fury, disruption of family life by the flight into Egypt, exile from their home in Bethlehem, and subsequent relocation in Nazareth, Luke's infancy narrative is a model of decorous progression through the fulfillment of ritual requirements of the faith by an orderly, stable family punctilious in Jewish Temple observance. The location of Jesus' birth is dictated by a decree from Caesar Augustus, with which the civic-minded Joseph complies despite his wife's advanced stage of pregnancy. Like John, Jesus is duly circumcised on the eighth day. When the time comes for Mary's purification, Jesus is presented in the Temple for the ritual redemption of the firstborn son; Luke's evocation of the delivery from bondage in Egypt conforms strictly to a traditional ritual pattern, unlike Matthew's literal reenactment. The Holy Spirit sends Simeon to the Temple to witness the presentation of Jesus, and inspires him to utter the Nunc Dimittis and prophesy doom over Jesus. Anna, an aged widow and prophet who has made her home in the Temple and her life a continuous act of worship there, also praises God for the child, although Luke gives us no record of her words. So Jesus, at the age of one month, acquires a Temple equivalent of a pair of godparents who, on his behalf, stake his first claim to a prominent role in the house of God. Further, Anna becomes Jesus' first publicist; she speaks openly about him in Jerusalem. Luke's infant Jesus poses no threat to Roman or Temple authorities. The Temple welcomes him in as a son.

Jesus' Moral Growth

Both Jesus' and John's early lives are characterized by careful and joyful Jewish ritual observance, and simultaneously by the Hellenistic concept of progress, *prokopto*, which encompasses moral, intellectual, physical, and emotional growth. This progress, as Luke applies it to Jesus and John, occurs in the context of the family and helps us to understand the life of the child in the family. We find this concept of progress in many Greek sources, including Josephus, who shows it actively operating in the context of a first-century Jewish family.

In his autobiography, Josephus describes his own upbringing by his devout father, Matthias, in Jerusalem. Josephus made great progress in education, which secured his reputation for an excellent memory and understanding. At fourteen he won universal accolades for his love of learning to the degree that the chief priests and leading men of the city came constantly to him for information on legal matters. Josephus's mention of his devout father, his own moral and spiritual growth, and his understanding demonstrate that while both Josephus and Jesus may have been prodigies, this pattern of education was common among children of the elite. The parallels are so clear between Josephus's account of his own education and Luke's account of Jesus' upbringing that we are allowed through Josephus to get a glimpse of what Jesus' education and adolescence were like, and what parents were expected to provide for their children by way of educational and developmental experience.

The use of the word *prokopto* places Luke in the mainstream of contemporary discussion about moral progress. It is another word unique to Luke among the Gospels, although it appears in Paul and other epistles. The noun *prokope* is a technical term in Stoic philosophy used to describe moral and spiritual growth. According to the Greek philosopher Chrysippus, the wise man is one who *progresses,* seemingly effortlessly, from folly to wisdom. Stoic writers used the term in the first century to describe "the progress toward virtue" (Epictetus), but Luke, Paul, and other early Christian writers did not necessarily draw from the Stoics; the idea was common in the surrounding culture. An epigraphical attestation, for example, in the Vibius Salutaris Inscription of 104 CE speaks of one "embellishing by his dignified behavior the progress toward betterment which Fortune has bestowed." A third- or fourth-century marble stele on the tomb of one Rufinus may allude to the advancement of his career: "Shining out in the progress he made, he provided many things for many people, causing distress to no one, but considered what was just."

By contrast with the somewhat tendentious Stoic concept of effortless and sudden progress, the more conservative Plutarch argues in his contemporaneous essay "How a Man May Become Aware of His Progress in Virtue" (*Moralia* 75–86) that one can measure progress by specific indications to which one would do well to pay attention, giving us further insight into the patterns by which families were expected to train their offspring. For example, an ability to conclude discussions without wrangling and boasting of success or anticipating applause are, Plutarch maintains, marks of progress. Luke's depiction of Jesus' development agrees more with Plutarch's understanding of progress and would appeal more to a conservative audience than the Stoic concept.

Jesus is brought to the Temple again by his parents at the age of twelve. Two summary statements bracket this episode: "The child grew and became strong, filled with wisdom; and the favor of God was upon him" (2:40) and "Jesus increased (*prokopto*) in wisdom and in years, and in divine and human favor" (2:52). The first statement bridges the time from infancy to this early adolescent moment, the second points to continuing progress in the same pattern. Between these two statements we find this unique episode where we see the growing Jesus engage with his parents and his vocation.

Luke portrays Jesus' parents as devout Jews who attend Passover in Jerusalem with Jesus, their extended family, and other relatives every year, indicating that such public accountability was an intrinsic part of family life. In the ancient world, public participation in the authorized religion was part of the household's responsibility in the civic forum as much as in the religious forum. We must remember that civic stability was thought to depend on correct and dutiful religious observance, and one of the charges brought against early Christian communities was atheism. In this episode, Luke demonstrates the civic responsibility of Jesus' family by showing their public attendance at the festival in the central place of worship, the Temple.

On this occasion, Jesus' enthusiasm for learning and the Torah leads him to stay behind in the Temple after his family leave, sitting with the teachers, listening and engaging in debate. Everyone there is amazed at his understanding and his answers. Jesus is portrayed not so much as a student but as an equal in learned debate.

Luke's account does not just display Jesus' intellectual progress; it also highlights Jesus' separation from his parents in physical, intellectual, and religious spheres. Extended families and neighbors traveled together, and children intermingled in the group; Jesus' absence is not noted for a full day's journey. His parents have another day's journey back to Jerusalem, and another day searching for him. To his parents, when they finally find him in the Temple, Jesus' spiritual and intellectual proficiency recedes into the background while his behavior toward them seems incomprehensible. His mother asks, "Child, why have you treated us like this? Look, your father and I have been searching for you in great anxiety!" "Did you not know that I must be in my Father's house?" is the explanation Jesus offers his parents for his three day absence. Actually, as the footnote in the NRSV text indicates, this text could be read in several ways, including, "Did you not know that I must be about my Father's interests?" This is a wonderful example of the Greek use of the article, "the" and the possessive form of "my father," so a truly idiomatic translation would read, "Do you not know I must be in [or 'among'] the whatever of my father?" The words *oikos* or *oikia* do not occur in the passage. The underlying Greek has been understood in various ways: perhaps "at my Father's place," namely, the Temple; or "that I must concern myself with my Father's affairs," literally, "the things of my Father." Perhaps the ambiguity is deliberate: this Father's affairs, after all, encompass everything. With these words, Jesus distances himself from his parents; we can imagine their dismay as he attaches himself to the heavenly Father. Jesus is setting one father in his life against the other, and privileging God over Joseph. His understanding may have increased but it is at their expense. He grows not with them but apart from them, both physically and intellectually. But the text closes up the gap, at least for the present; Luke immediately shows Jesus returning into the domain of his earthly parents, in dutiful subjection: "Then he went down with them and came to Nazareth, and was obedient to them" (2:51). Luke stresses that this rupture and reconciliation is in God's plan, for the narrative concludes with the observation that Jesus grew "in wisdom and in years, and in divine and human favor."

Jesus' response to his parents when they find him in the Jerusalem Temple confirms that Luke understands moral and intellectual
growth to occur and to be measurable along lines similar to
Plutarch's description. While Jesus' parents may fail to compre-
hend his progress, Luke shows that Jesus gives them no cause for
distress, for Jesus responds to them with courtesy and deference,
and is obedient to them. Theophilus and Luke's readers perceive
accordingly Jesus' quantifiable advance from adolescence to maturity. In so presenting Jesus, Luke demonstrates an understanding
of moral progress, *prokopto,* closely tied to the family setting,
where stability, quiet, and order provide the ground for Jesus to
progress to maturity. Luke's portrait of family life shows us what
might have been expected of the household that gives rise to a
great religious and spiritual leader, which therefore also provides
the pattern for the households of his followers. The thing that
makes Luke's account of Jesus' progress distinctive from other
biographical material such as Josephus's *Life* is the fact that it is
situated not just in the home of Jesus, but rather in the separation, or perhaps the tension, between the parents' house and the
house of God.

At the beginning of the episode, the parents are the primary
actors in the scene; by the end, Jesus has taken charge of events,
even though the account concludes with his dutiful subjection to
his parents. What is going on here? Does Luke's narrative shift,
from parents to Jesus, suggest that Jesus' ministry and devotion
to God will mystify his family of origin? Luke does not describe
Jesus' parents as being present during the course of his ministry,
although Mary reappears in Jerusalem with Jesus' brothers at the
beginning of Acts. Luke describes Mary's response to the distanc-
ing by saying she "keeps all these things in her heart," as Tyndale
renders 2:51. The Greek verb connotes preserving something
with an implication of duration: it describes Jacob's reflection
on Joseph's dreams in Genesis 37:11 and frequently refers to preserving or keeping God's laws. Mary treasures these events for
future reflection; she may not understand her son, but she does

not dismiss what he says. Instead she continues to ponder his words. Luke describes separation but not severance between parents and child. It is the kind of scene of which an elite Roman male like Theophilus would approve, emphasizing Roman family values and the education and moral growth of boys with potential separation from the mother.

Luke describes this whole movement of separation and differentiation as moral and spiritual growth sanctioned by God, as well as by Hellenistic society. Jesus pursues his own intellectual and moral growth apart from his parents by conversing as an equal with religious leaders. When he goes home with his earthly parents he returns to a subordinate relationship with them, proving that his absence was not the product of adolescent rebellion but appropriate growth.

The difficult sayings of Jesus that predict conflict between family members and demand rejection of family ties appear in Matthew, Mark, and Luke, a phenomenon scholars call "triple attestation" and interpret as clearly pointing to source material that could not be glossed over or ignored. Each Gospel writer presents this material in a way consistent with the points that writer is trying to make about Jesus, but however nuanced, these sayings offend and challenge the sensibilities of a world where the family is the basic unit for civic and religious responsibility. In this episode with the adolescent Jesus, Luke lays the groundwork in the Gospel for Jesus to move away from his family of origin into behavior in accord with God's plan. The stage is set in Luke, and a pattern established, which will ameliorate somewhat the harshness of these sayings. When in 8:20–21 Jesus identifies his mother and brothers as those who hear the word of God and do it, and rejects his biological family, or when he describes a mission as bringing division in a household, father against son and son against father in 12:52–53, readers of Luke may now be able to recognize that such words are not expected to undermine family values in a Roman world, but instead indicate healthy separation of disciples from their families following Jesus' model and serving the purposes of God.

Luke's Urbane Households

Luke's interest in families and houses is not restricted to the opening chapters: in fact, the entire Gospel uses a larger vocabulary for houses, households, and buildings than Matthew, Mark, or John (see Appendix). This can be partly accounted for by recognizing that Luke is so much bigger. Each of the other Gospels stands alone as a discreet single volume work, but Luke is part one of a two-volume work, Luke-Acts. The author dedicates both works to the same single putative reader, Theophilus, and the Acts of the Apostles opens with a reference to "the former treatise" — Luke's Gospel — detailing the life and acts of Jesus. Luke and Acts are the longest books in the New Testament, each filling a scroll of thirty-one or thirty-two feet in length. A manageable scroll could be no longer than thirty-five feet, so Luke was pushing the publishing limits of his time with each treatise. Since the Gospel of Luke and the Acts of the Apostles were written as companion works, it is useful to read Luke with an eye to Acts and Acts with an eye to Luke, and to treat the two documents as two volumes of a single work.

Luke's larger vocabulary about households reflects Luke's concern to recognize households as units of civic responsibility in Hellenistic cities. Over half of the instances of the word *polis,* city or town, in the New Testament occur in Luke-Acts. Luke locates households within urban settings that only he identifies as cities. For example, in the Gospel and in Acts, Luke identifies Bethsaida, Capernaum, and Nazareth by the term *polis* when other contemporaneous writers identify them as villages, *komes,* not cities. Just as our cities include resources one might not find in a smaller municipality, like a courthouse, a department store, or a symphony hall, a Hellenistic city contained a number of public places such as the *agora* (marketplace), the gymnasium, and the public arena. In these places citizens met and households participated in their obligations of civic service and public life. Philippi, for example, is identified by Luke in Acts 16 as a Roman colony and a *polis* open to the countryside through gates outside one of which is a place of prayer. There is an *agora* where magistrates hear cases, and a prison with solid foundations. A *polis* will have a law enforcement presence, the centurion and his troops. Bethlehem, Luke implies, is a city of sufficient prominence to make it a place where births records are maintained and a census may be recorded, which provides the reason for Luke to make it the setting for Jesus' birth; the Gospel of John calls Bethlehem a village, *kome*. So Luke prefers to present households in the context of a larger civic setting with more opportunities for engagement in the public arena than might be implied if villages and towns were not upgraded by his vocabulary to cities. This may be a way to enhance the importance of the emerging movement to Theophilus, but it also shows both Theophilus and us that households in Luke were expected to participate in the civic duties of their cities.

Members of Luke's households not only participated actively in the city, but also belonged to voluntary associations. We are told in Luke 5:10 that James, John, and Simon were partners in the fishing business. Families in the same trade often formed business associations or cartels together, where several persons in each family might be active members of the association. Ancient voluntary associations included many of the same features we find in modern unions: a common fund is maintained which may be used for the welfare of the needy, rules must be observed, protocols for entering into and being expelled from the association exist, and members consider themselves and address each other as brothers. Modern unions don't usually include provision for sacrifices to a patron deity, but even today there are some voluntary associations with significant religious components. Luke's households would have participated in voluntary professional associations which extend the language of family into the business arena. So it is possible that Luke considers the voluntary association, where members are called by sibling language, more of a model for his emerging community in Acts than the family or household unit.

Unlike Matthew, Luke makes no effort to redefine the family or household in such a way that it becomes a new template for community. When Luke recounts the episode where Jesus commands someone to follow him, and the potential disciple asks to defer until he has buried his father, the story is embedded in a series of injunctions about the urgency of proclaiming the gospel (9:57–62). The context of the saying makes it clear that Luke's interest is not in the displacement of the human father in favor of the heavenly one, as we find in Matthew; for Luke, what matters about this saying is that following Jesus takes priority over every other consideration, overriding even the obligations of family and household.

Because of this, Luke does acknowledge that the call to discipleship and adherence to Jesus will result in conflict within families. In the divided five-person household described by Jesus in Luke 12:52–53 (cf. Matthew 10:35–36), conflicts run on both gender and generational lines. The presence of a daughter-in-law defines the household as an extended family, in this particular case constituted by mother, father, son, daughter, and daughter-in-law. Jesus says he has come to bring division through three distinct lines of conflict: "From now on five in one household will be divided, three against two and two against three; they will be divided: father against son and son against father, mother against daughter and daughter against mother, mother-in-law against daughter-in-law and daughter-in-law against mother-in-law." Neither the mother-father couple nor the son–daughter-in-law couple is described as husband and wife; the siblings are not described as brother and sister; all participants are identified solely by the role they play in the dividing conflict. The conflict seems to run along intergenerational lines, but we cannot be certain which generation would be following Jesus; the father or mother might be the one leaving the household to be a disciple against the son or daughter or daughter-in-law's protest, or vice versa. The aspiring disciples might be sons like James and John, the sons of Zebedee, or the son who wished to bury his father, or they might be daughters or wives. No matter which member of the family is following Jesus, a state of conflict within households will be a continuing condition; Jesus introduces the passage with the phrase "From now on. . . ."

Luke returns to the theme of intra-family conflict later. In Luke 14:26, Jesus declares emphatically that whoever comes to him and does not hate father and mother, wife and children, brothers and sisters, and even life itself cannot be his disciple. The saying comes in a series of strong, startling admonitions and is directly followed by the saying "Whoever does not carry the cross and follow me cannot be my disciple." Immediately preceding the saying about hating father and mother is the story of the great banquet. In this story, the host sends out invitations to a great banquet and then, when the time has come for the banquet, sends his slave to summon the guests. The guests now beg off with a variety of excuses related to their households: the need to inspect some livestock, the recent acquisition of a piece of land, having recently been married. The host declares that none of these no-shows will taste the banquet, and populates the table with the disenfranchised, those who have no property or family obligations.

This story serves two functions: the first part depicts the problems that family ties present to those who would participate in the heavenly banquet; Jesus concludes the story with the saying that those who would follow him must hate father, mother, wife, children, life itself. In the second part, Jesus teaches that invitations to a meal should be extended not to friends, brothers, rich neighbors, or relatives who can reciprocate, but to the poor, the crippled, the lame, and the blind, those who cannot repay you, the principle intrinsic to Luke's understanding of hospitality. The responses given by those who excuse themselves from the banquet indicate that this story presupposes the individual male disciple of the middle generation with a father and mother, brothers and sisters, a wife and children in a household. A middle generation married man would reject his obligations and privileges in the household to follow Jesus, thus becoming one of the disenfranchised preferred by Jesus. So here the individual follower of Jesus is not a house-holder who can extend hospitality, but one of those who needs it and cannot reciprocate. In the abandoned *oikos*, fathers remain as heads of households while sons leave to become disciples.

What does it mean to hate one's family and life? The language of the injunction is strong, and has caused distress through centuries. An easy solution is to dismiss it, as well as the language about carrying one's cross, as hyperbole, exaggeration, or meta-phor. But the fact that such strong language is reiterated several times in one short passage, the relentless exclusion of those who use family ties and responsibilities as an excuse not to respond, and the call to carry the cross, suggest that we must try to make some sense of it. The subsequent stories about counting the cost before committing to a course of action suggest that we must be prepared to accept the most difficult consequences of our choice to follow Jesus. We are to love our enemies; we are to hate those who stand in the way of our following Jesus, even if they are father, mother, brother, sister, wife, children, our own life. The household must not divert us from following Jesus.

The household should instead serve as a context for provid-ing a "great banquet" and modeling the forgiving love of God the Father. In the parable of the prodigal son (or the loving fa-ther), the elder son remains in the household, while the younger son takes his inheritance and departs. The younger son's action is tantamount to declaring his father dead; an heir does not inherit prior to the death of the testator. The parable shows a positive opinion of the father and his household, but not of either of the two sons. It proposes a situation in which the traditional house-hold has to accept into itself the one who left it for dead and who thus has threatened its existence; the taking and squandering of the inheritance has reduced the household assets by the younger son's portion. We have heard this parable so often it is easy to underrate the impact of the younger son's actions: the diminished family estate must continue to provide for the entire household, and as we know from the presence of slaves, this is a large and extended household with significant responsibilities. Not only do the immediate family members depend upon the continuance of this household, slaves and all those who provide services to the household are affected by this untimely reduction of the estate. Where the part taken by the younger son should have continued to increase the estate's net worth until the time of the father's real death, and thus provide even greater security and stability for the household and its attendants, now everyone's resources are straitened. The son has clearly not counted the cost of this action. This parable demonstrates a son hating his father, but not in order to follow Jesus, only to indulge himself. There is in Jesus' teaching no condoning of cavalier disrespect for the father and household. Destitute, the son ultimately returns home in the hope of honest employment. There he finds himself restored to his former status through the ungrudging forgiveness of the father. The older brother is, understandably, piqued. The father reassures the older brother that everything he has now belongs to the older brother, and exhorts the older brother to rejoice, because "this brother of yours was dead and has come to life; he was lost and has been found." Note the reversal here; the younger son, by claiming the inheritance, effectively declared the father dead; and yet it is the father who has mourned the younger son as the dead one. Far from displacing the human father in the household, as Matthew does, Luke requires that the human father demonstrate the love and unconditional forgiveness of the heavenly Father in the most difficult of circumstances. The call to follow Jesus may require one to "hate one's children" in some circumstances; but in others, the hearts of the fathers must turn to the children, as prophesied at the birth of John the Baptist.

A similar restoration to household occurs in 8:27–39, where a demoniac, whom Luke describes as living not in a house but in uncivilized and contaminated tombs, receives healing from Jesus and subsequently asks to stay with him. Jesus tells the healed man to return to his *oikos* and to spread the word about Jesus from that place. Here the one who has been deprived of house and household by illness is restored by the call of Jesus not only to health, but also to mission and to his household as a base for that mission. Following Jesus may not, in fact, entail hating family or home or life, but rather being returned to all these things and turning them to the service of Jesus. The restored household is the context from which the mission may be advanced.

When men are called to leave their households and become disciples, their wives are abandoned with the household. In 18:28–9 Peter protests that the disciples have left households to follow Jesus, and Jesus' response implies that wives are among the abandoned members of those households. In the parable of the great banquet, one of the invitees uses his recent wedding as an excuse not to attend the banquet. (Being in the first year of a marriage excused one automatically from a number of social obligations, like military service.)

Similarly, sometimes the wife seems to leave the husband behind, as in the case of Joanna. Luke 8:1–3 describes Jesus' itinerant mission as being financially underwritten and accompanied by women who had been healed by him. Mary Magdalene, of course, is included, but two others are mentioned by name among "many others," Joanna the wife of Herod's steward Chuza, and Susanna. The mentioning of people by name suggests that these persons are well known to the community and to the intended audience. This is certainly the case with Susanna, who appears nowhere else in the New Testament, and about whom we know nothing beyond what Luke implies here, that she was sufficiently affluent to make a financial contribution to the mission, sufficiently free of household responsibilities to accompany the mission, sufficiently healthy to serve. Joanna in her own right was not so well known, and in this we are fortunate, because we learn who her husband was. Luke was name-dropping; the word used for "steward" here, *epitropos,* suggests a person of significant rank, a governor, overseer, or high-ranking administrator, with either economic or political authority in Herod's domain, attached to his private estate or appointed over a political district. Does Luke mention Chuza because Theophilus, the addressee of the Gospel, knows him, or because Chuza is an elite male whose rank will impress, or are there other possible implications? Joanna is a continuing member of the mission, and is mentioned by name as a witness to the resurrection (24:10). Has Joanna separated from Chuza? If Joanna follows the mission as a woman who has separated from her husband, then perhaps Luke is emphasizing the magnitude of personal sacrifice which disciples are willing to make; but then where is Joanna getting the resources she is using to support the mission? Independently wealthy women did exist in Jesus' world, but one of the socio-economic reasons for opposition to divorce was the destitution it often imposed on a divorced woman. Another possibility is that Joanna has not, in fact, separated from her husband, but has gone on mission with Chuza's permission or perhaps even under his direction. Luke may be implying that Chuza the steward of Herod approves of the mission sufficiently to be willing to endorse his wife's participation and undergo the consequent deprivation. However things stand with Chuza, Joanna, unlike other disciples, is not described as having left anything; she remains "the wife of Chuza."

Householders like Levi the tax collector (and collaborator with Rome) are called to follow Jesus, which entails leaving but not necessarily giving up their households. While Luke records that Levi responded to Jesus' invitation to follow him by getting up, "leaving everything," and following him, the next verse (5:29) states that Levi gave a great banquet for Jesus in his house. So in the case of Levi, "everything" cannot be construed to include his house and household. One might infer, of course, that without the livelihood derived from tax collecting, Levi would ultimately be forced to surrender his household; or one might conjecture that Levi waited until after the banquet to put his property up for sale, or deeded it over to his offspring so he could follow Jesus unencumbered; but if we take Luke's text at face value, the implication is that Levi's house and household became part of the common resources of the community that followed Jesus, even though Levi himself joined the itinerant mission.

Finally, supportive householders are not always required to leave their house and accompany Jesus in order to be disciples. Zacchaeus, in Luke 19, expresses interest in Jesus by climbing a tree so he can see him pass by. Jesus invites himself to stay at Zacchaeus's house, and when Zacchaeus hears some of the onlookers criticize Jesus for consorting with tax collectors, he voluntarily offers to repay fourfold those whom he has defrauded, and give half his possessions to the poor. The story never suggests that Zacchaeus is asked to give up his household. Perhaps Zacchaeus is left with some of his wealth in order to provide for other followers of Jesus needing future hospitality.

Hospitality and Table Fellowship

In contrast to Matthew, in Luke Jesus has no house of his own. In the early part of the Gospel, Jesus preaches in towns around Galilee like Nazareth and Capernaum, where he visits houses of disciples like Simon and Levi, and local officials like the Pharisee in Luke 7. In Jerusalem, Jesus probably rents the upper room used for the Last Supper. After the resurrection, Jesus stays again with disciples in Emmaus. In the early part of chapter 9, the twelve disciples are sent out on missionary sorties, practicing their skills at spreading the word and receiving hospitality. But the middle of the Gospel includes a long section that begins in chapter 9:51 and ends in Jerusalem, usually called the "travel section" of Luke. In these chapters, Jesus and the disciples who accompany him and who sometimes go off in pairs are entirely dependent on the hospitality they can find as they travel. In this section we see the broad range of hospitality offered or withheld, and observe Jesus' assumptions about hospitality revealed, usually peripherally to the main point, in his stories and sayings. So too, Jesus tells the twelve to accept others' hospitality (9:4), and in fact not to move from house to house but to settle down for a while and be accepted by the householders. These glimpses of hospitality, mostly provided by households, demonstrate another facet of the responsibilities attendant upon households and householders.

Jesus' own practice and his instructions to disciples presume that households of the time practice hospitality, and we generally subscribe to a belief that in the Middle East of Jesus' time the demands of hospitality were universally recognized and honored. Jesus tells the story of the sleeping father who rises in the middle of the night to respond to his friend's need (11:5–8) with the stated purpose of illustrating persistence in prayer; the father responds so that the friend will stop knocking and he and his family can go back to sleep. But this story also reveals strong presuppositions about hospitality: the friend's need rises out of the arrival of an unexpected traveling visitor who must be welcomed and fed, no matter how inconvenient the time or circumstances. The evidence indicates, however, that not every traveler received a welcome, and thus not every householder of the time honored or felt the obligations of hospitality. Twice the disciples are instructed about what to do in the event that they are refused hospitality (9:5; 10:10–12). Further, while Jesus assumes that those who request hospitality should receive it, Jesus enjoins his disciples to volunteer hospitality only to those who cannot reciprocate.

Luke describes a variety of houses in this travel section detailing Jesus' journey to Jerusalem. Large houses, or villas, appear in the story of a proprietor who has a steward (*oikonomos*) in Luke 16:1–8, in the parable of the great banquet (14:7–24), and the house of the rich man at whose gate Lazarus sits daily, begging and ignored (16:19–21). Rich men live in large houses run by household managers, but these parables tell of obsession with wealth and immediate family to the exclusion of ordinary demands of hospitality and charity toward neighbors. Lazarus the beggar at the rich man's gate couldn't be a much closer neighbor, but the rich man cannot see him in this life. When the rich man arrives in the place of damnation and Lazarus is sitting in Abraham's bosom, the rich man still perceives Lazarus only as a means to the end of saving his own family, his brothers.

Medium-sized houses include that of the householder who probably has only a single slave to carry out all the household tasks, including work in the fields and serving meals (17:7–9). Martha and Mary's small house seems to contain no slaves as Martha herself is busy with household tasks and assumes Mary will join her in doing the work required to welcome Jesus as guest. In fact, the household of Mary and Martha is entirely made up of siblings. Luke's account of the father who gets up in the middle of the night to provide bread for his neighbor perhaps suggests poorer houses crowded close together, row or apartment houses such as we find in the largest urban areas. While the homes of the respectably wealthy are deficient in their responsibilities of hospitality, Jesus is shown hospitality by those in medium-sized, small, and poor houses. Those homes where there is evidence of significant wealth show hospitality to Jesus when the householder is in some other way ostracized or marginalized, like Zacchaeus.

So far we have seen hospitality extended, as would be expected, from the site of family life, the house and household. Jesus' special commands regarding hospitality move it beyond the ordinary context of reciprocal hospitality into a context where special rules operate, where the guests of choice are those who cannot reciprocate, where the marginalized and ostracized are brought into the sphere of family and household life in response to Jesus' teaching regarding hospitality. Similarly, Luke extends the sites for the exercise of hospitality to include inns. When the inn is full at Bethlehem in the birth narrative, the inn's stable provides shelter for the newborn child and his parents, becoming a temporary house for the transient family. Another special Lukan parable, the good Samaritan, describes extending kinship and hospitality to the marginalized beyond the boundaries of Israel. Jesus tells this story to a questioner who tries to limit the scope of selfless love by precisely identifying who is one's neighbor. The story turns the question around; it is not the status of neighbor that entitles one to compassion, but the exercise of compassion that identifies one as neighbor. The priest and Levite, both of whom might have been considered kin and neighbor by virtue of sharing descent from Jacob (Israel) and common religious observance, love themselves and their ritual purity more than the human victim who needs them, and so they exclude themselves from the status of neighbor. The despised Samaritan exercises compassion and hospitality toward the victim who fell among thieves, and thus becomes neighbor and kinsperson. So too, the exercise of unreciprocated hospitality by households toward the marginalized and needy brings the recipients of this hospitality into the family domain of the hosts.

An intrinsic element of hospitality is the providing of food, and Luke shows Jesus dining at the homes of others in terms that would be easily recognizable to his audience, Theophilus. In Luke, Jesus frequently discusses the Law and teaches while a guest at a meal in someone else's house. Theophilus would recognize this kind of meal as a symposium, a philosophical discourse that takes place in a dining room, along the pattern of Plato's *Symposium*, in which a meal became the setting for a discourse on love (*eros*). The symposium had a prescribed pattern both of discussion and of eating, and a communicated order, reminding us that one of the stated purposes of Luke's Gospel is to present an "orderly account." The entire chapter of Luke 14 is a description of such a symposium. In it, we see assembled those who would normally be present on such an occasion: the host or master of the house (one of the chief Pharisees), the guest of honor or the main speaker (Jesus), and other invited and uninvited guests. The semipublic nature of the household is evident from the outset; this meal is at a Pharisee's home on the Sabbath, but right at the beginning of the meal a person (an uninvited guest) appears for healing. Jesus presents the issue as a subject for discussion: is it lawful to heal on the Sabbath? The Pharisees decline to take up the issue; Jesus heals the person and justifies the healing to his hosts. The symposium continues with Jesus' instruction on the etiquette of attending symposia: guests should recline at low status places at the table, and allow their hosts to raise them higher, rather than open themselves to the shame of being asked to move to lower places. (Modern translations use "sit down," but the Greek uses the verb "recline," the correct posture for eating at a formal meal of the well-educated and well-bred.) Jesus then enjoins those present to invite to their banquets those who cannot reciprocate, and thereby receive recompense at the resurrection of the righteous. A questioner encourages Jesus to continue discussing the heavenly banquet. Jesus responds with the story of the great banquet. With its chilling final declaration, "none of those who were invited shall taste my dinner," Jesus turns toward the crowds who waiting outside, and continues to teach with his saying on family conflict. Here Jesus effectively opens the symposium to the marginalized. Thus the house and household are presented as an appropriate site for philosophical and religious discussion and instruction, and providing a place for such discussion is an intrinsic responsibility of the well-regulated household.

In homes that were able to offer banquets, these symposia would be served by household servants or slaves. Luke presents the Last Supper (22:14–38) as a symposium taking place in a rented room, and here Jesus takes the role of the table servant, making himself a model for community service. The one who has the right to the highest seat adopts the role of the lowest servant. The group of disciples becomes the household that hosts the meal which will become the central expression of the community's life together.

The next time we see Jesus at table, the disciples are shown practicing the hospitality they have been taught. On the road to Emmaus (24:13–32), a stranger has fallen in with them. He does not know what has happened in Jerusalem, but the disciples fill him in, and tell him that some women saw angels who said Jesus is alive. The unrecognized Jesus instructs them along the road, and they press him to stay with them for the night. At supper, he blesses the bread, they recognize them, and he vanishes. Here Luke adds an incentive for hospitality to strangers: any stranger to whom they offer hospitality might be the resurrected Lord.

For Luke, the household and family provide a base for spreading the word about the kingdom. They are the place where children are raised to serve as prophets and disciples, where fathers turn their hearts to children and provide according to the model of God providing for his children, where traveling disciples find shelter and food, where scripture is expounded and righteous behavior taught and understood. And, going forward into Luke's second volume, we find that they become the place for community worship.

From Temple to House

Acts begins with an address to Theophilus, reminding him of the purpose of the first volume, the Gospel. Both the Gospel and Acts open with works of the Holy Spirit; Luke describes the child John the Baptist as a prophet in the spirit and power of Elijah, and explains Jesus' conception in Mary as occurring by means of the Spirit. Acts begins with an account of the gift of tongues through the Spirit to the assembled believers so that they might witness "to the ends of the earth." Thus, it is the Holy Spirit in Luke and Acts that both engenders the child Jesus and brings the community into being.

Both works begin in Jerusalem, and the Gospel ends in Jerusalem. At the beginning of the Gospel Zechariah is officiating in the Jerusalem Temple (God's house) when the angel of the Lord appears to him at the right side of the altar, and Jerusalem is where the believers are assembled when the Spirit descends upon their heads at the beginning of Acts. At the beginning of Jesus' life, his parents take him to be circumcised in Jerusalem, and it is in Jerusalem that Jesus is crucified. It is from Jerusalem at the beginning of Acts that the good news will be taken to the ends of the earth by Philip and the other apostles, and at the end of Acts, to Rome by Paul. Jerusalem functions as a pivotal locus linking the end of the Gospel with the beginning of Acts. Luke the writer has a developed theology of urban place: Jerusalem is the center of the universe and the place of death and life. In the Gospel, Jesus' prophetic life begins in the Temple when he is twelve, and in Acts the prophetic life of the community begins with daily prayer and worship in the Temple. The house of God serves as the household of origin for the believing community.

Luke makes this point for Theophilus in Acts, but we must remember that by the time Luke has written the Gospel and Acts, the Temple in Jerusalem is only a memory, and there is no longer a central place to worship. It has become difficult to recognize that the believers in Jesus are fulfilling their civic responsibilities of worship because much of the worship life has moved into households, semipublic places rather than the centralized locus for worship in the Temple. Luke uses the flow of movement from Temple to household and back in the Gospel and in Acts to demonstrate the public accountability of believing families.

At the beginning of Acts, Luke inserts frequent narrative remarks on the increase of numbers in the Jerusalem community. These asides are in the third person — the same style used to comment on Jesus' moral and spiritual growth in Luke. Modern chapter and verse breaks, artificially imposed on what would have been the continuous script of the scroll of Acts, obscure the fact that the location of the narrative comments on the growth of the community in Acts exactly parallel the location of Luke's comments on Jesus' growth in the Gospel. The early household of Acts functions for the emerging Christian community in the same way as the family of Jesus in the Gospel functions for the emerging Lord of that community. Thus the early life of the Acts community may serve as a place where we can learn about Luke's family values.

Luke describes the growing community in Jerusalem moving between the two locations of Temple and house to worship and break bread together in just the same way that Jesus moved between Temple and house according to Luke 2. Each day, the text reports, as the Jerusalem community spent time together in the Temple, they broke bread at home (or, "from house to house"). There are textual variants here: Codex Bezae, for example, renders the verse thus: "All were regular in attendance at the Temple and in their homes were together."

Whatever way we read the verse, early Jerusalem believers moved between Temple and house. What is the relationship of Temple and house? Perhaps this is an indication of more formal public and less formal private worship. Some think that more formal worship was going on in the Temple and more private activities like eating and breaking bread were going on at home. Perhaps it is an indication that the community in Acts had not separated from the Temple. Perhaps worship (including breaking of bread in a context of eating) in houses is a satellite activity to public worship in the Temple. In Acts 8, Saul is described as ravaging the church (scattered community of believers) in Jerusalem and elsewhere by entering house after house. The Greek here is a plural form of the accusative "house" used in the same way as the singular in Acts 2:46, indicating "house to house." In the early part of the Gospel, Jesus moves back and forth from house to Temple, and in the early part of Acts the community moves back and forth from house to Temple.

By creating an analogy between Jesus' moral and spiritual growth and the increase and growth of the early community in Jerusalem, Luke provides readers with a tool for self-understanding and a connection to the time when the community was able to present itself in the public and civic exercise of accountability in the Temple. Further, the analogy to Jesus' movement out of his household of origin and into the larger arena sanctions the expansion that Acts describes from Jerusalem to the ends of the earth through the agencies of various apostles and missionary workers and with varying degrees of success. In Luke, the household of Jesus' family provides a template for the household of the

Jerusalem — and ultimately much wider — believing community in Acts.

The same Spirit that at the beginning of Luke quickened the children in the wombs of women in their house, at the beginning of Acts quickens the community of believers in a house that is not the Temple in Jerusalem. The place where the Spirit dwells, the house of God, moves from the Temple into the household of believers. So in the community of Acts we see a network of households, acting with public accountability, providing hospitality without reciprocation, and being a locus for worship, teaching, ministry, and sharing of resources. Thus the household provides the orderly and respectable foundation for the mission of the disciples to the ends of the earth, and Theophilus can be assured that these followers of Jesus are responsible and respectable participants for the public good.

Luke's ability to persuade authorities that the followers of Jesus presented no threat to the civilized order met with varying degrees of success in the first centuries of Christianity. But it must be noted that by the middle of the second century Luke's program for unreciprocated hospitality was so effective that the satirist Lucian wrote *The Passing of Peregrinus,* an essay mocking Christians for their undiscriminating liberality to the needy, which has rendered them vulnerable to exploitation by the unscrupulous. Luke offers no challenge to the basic structure of family or household, but calls them to become a base to provide the world with a challenge to the system of mutual reciprocity that kept the wealthy and the poor in separate spheres. Thus the hospitality of households in Luke worked to reshape the world in the likeness of the kingdom of heaven.

Chapter Five

PAUL'S URBAN HOUSEHOLDS

DURING THE COURSE of Paul's travels, Luke records, it was possible for a demon to say, "Jesus I know, and Paul I know, but who are you?" to the sons of Sceva, who were trying to exorcise him in the name of "the Jesus whom Paul proclaims" (Acts 19:13–16). Paul preached and wrote before the Gospels were written, and for a large number of those who believed in Jesus, it was the Jesus Paul proclaimed whom they knew. Paul mentions in his letters other evangelists who were spreading the word, but for the most part they didn't leave any letters for us. The undisputed letters of Paul are the earliest witness to communities of those who believed in Jesus Christ, so if we want to know how family values were reflected in those communities, Paul is where we must start.

Many people know Paul only through one text in the Bible that is often read at weddings — his sermon on love in 1 Corinthians 13. (Ephesians, another epistle popular at weddings, is attributed to Paul but was not written by him.) And where does this sermon appear in the context of Paul's letters? It lies embedded in a sequence of community teaching about care for "the weaker brethren" and has nothing to do with marriage. The one place Paul does address marriage, 1 Corinthians 7, is significantly absent from the texts to be read at wedding services. The use of 1 Corinthians 13 over 1 Corinthians 7 reflects the church's understanding that Paul wrote different kinds of texts, and some of them are theologically significant while others are ad hoc advice to particular circumstances arising in particular places.

"I Do, I Do!"

The phrase "I do" signifies marriage in the world of plays and movies, but no bride or groom ever says "I do" in weddings from the Book of Common Prayer. There the question is "Will you have this man/woman to be your husband/wife. . . . Will you love, honor, cherish . . . " and so forth, and the answer is "I will." Real marriage doesn't happen in a moment; it is concerned with the long haul, the future. The earliest Christian communities hoped and believed fervently that there wasn't going to *be* much of a future, and so Paul, our best witness to such communities, doesn't have a burning interest in marriage; he considers marriage the only acceptable alternative to burning (uncontrolled sexual desire). And we have seen that Jesus and the Gospels have similarly little interest in marriage, other than prohibiting divorce.

It's a curious irony that promoters of "traditional family values" which they consider "countercultural" in today's world are drawing their standards from sections of scripture that are most interested in making ancient Christian communities appear more acceptable to the world they inhabited. From the end of the first century CE onward, as Christianity became differentiated from Judaism in the public eye, and thereby lost the special status that exempted Jews from state religion, Christian communities came under attack for perceived impiety and moral turpitude. Clearly the relatively egalitarian nature of the communities drew fire from neighbors around. The later epistles, which although ascribed to Paul were not written by him, reflect this with significant passages on marriage and household clearly addressed at biological families.

At the core of the current family values debate lies our understanding of the purpose and nature of marriage. How did we get from a time where marriage was an interim solution while we awaited the imminent arrival of the Last Judgment, to a world where, according to the preamble to the marriage service, "marriage signifies the mystery of the union between Christ and his Church"?

For many, Paul's teaching about marriage and related matters in 1 Corinthians 7 is clear, authoritative, and Christian. Peter Brown, in his book *The Body and Society,* describes it as the one chapter that was to determine all Christian thought on marriage and celibacy for well over a millennium. At the same time, he characterizes it as "distinctly lopsided" because it reflects Paul's concern not so much to praise marriage as to point out that marriage was safer than unconsidered celibacy. What's going on?

In trying to understand Paul, I take consolation from the author of 2 Peter 3:16, who describes some things in Paul's letters as "hard to understand." Perhaps this reflects difficulties early readers had in interpreting Paul. If near contemporaries had trouble grasping what Paul meant, how much more might we?

For centuries people understood Paul to be of the opinion that marriage was second best and celibacy a higher calling. Better not to give expression to sexual desires lest they distract from service of God. The second- or third-century noncanonical Acts of Paul, unconstrained by notions of an impending apocalyptic crisis, actually went so far as to portray Paul's ascetic preaching from 1 Corinthians 7 in the style of Jesus in Matthew's Sermon on the Mount: "Blessed are the pure in heart, for they shall see God. Blessed are they who have kept the flesh pure, for they shall become a temple of God. Blessed are they who have wives as if they had them not, for they shall be heirs to God." This early portrait of Paul commending continence and sexual purity is not an unwarranted anomaly in Pauline interpretation but a justifiable reading of Paul's clear preference.

In 401, Augustine, having read Paul, wrote in *The Excellence of Marriage* that while it is good to bear children, not marrying is better because to have no need of this task is better for human society. He concludes, "It seems to me, therefore, that at the present time the only ones who should marry are those who are unable to be continent, in accordance with the advice of the apostle: 'If they are unable to be continent, they should marry; for it is better to marry then to burn (1 Cor. 7:9).'" Augustine's summary of Paul's teaching on marriage is reflected in different sources: centuries later, Chaucer's Wife of Bath, for example, says:

> This is the sum: [Paul] held virginity
> Nearer perfection than marriage for frailty.

Recent interpreters, however, have been claiming that far from promoting celibacy, a careful reading of 1 Corinthians 7 in context indicates that Paul is best understood as an advocate of marriage. Before reviewing a contemporary debate about whether Paul's arguments have or have not denigrated sexuality and whether Paul has been misunderstood, I want to make my own position clear. Paul's discussion about marriage and related matters has very little to do with his reading of what Jesus might have said or done. True, he knows of a command from the Lord that married people should not divorce, but this is not binding: in the next breath, he considers what to do if the woman does separate from her husband. Paul's discussion of marriage, divorce, and celibacy in 1 Corinthians 7 is not given as a theological position paper. Rather, the whole section occurs within a wider context of imminent apocalyptic crisis. Paul describes the time in which he writes as constricted (or compressed, rather than "grown short") because "the form of this world is passing away" (1 Cor. 7:29, 31). In view of imminent catastrophe, he advises not devoting much energy to worldly affairs. My understanding of Paul, like Paul's understanding of his time, is of course provisional. All any of us can do is give our best efforts to the task of biblical interpretation. If this discussion provokes us to further dialogue, even vehement discussion, so much the better. What do we know about Paul himself and his knowledge of Jesus before we turn to specific passages about families and households?

Authentic Letters of Paul

The authentic Pauline letters were certainly written sometime before the Gospels. The Gospel of Mark was probably written about the time of the fall of Jerusalem in 70 CE or slightly before, Matthew and Luke perhaps in the mid-70s, and John's Gospel and epistles perhaps as late as 90–100. So our earliest window into Jesus and family values might well be the letters of Paul.

Of the thirteen epistles attributed to Paul in the New Testament, namely, Romans through Philemon, scholars agree that the apostle Paul of Tarsus indisputably wrote seven. Starting at about 49 CE, within fifteen years of the death of Jesus, 1 Thessalonians is thought to be the earliest text we have in the New Testament. Paul died around or shortly after the year 60. His authentic letters are 1 Thessalonians, Galatians, 1 and 2 Corinthians, Philippians, Philemon, and Romans, listed in very tenuous chronological order.

Colossians would have been written in the same time period if it were Paul's work, or a decade or two later (70–80 CE) if not; the scholarly debate on the authorship of Colossians is too close to call, but I find the arguments against Pauline authorship persuasive. The consensus on Ephesians attributes it to a close colleague or disciple of Paul who modeled it on Colossians, which would place it slightly later. The so-called Pastoral Epistles, 1 and 2 Timothy and Titus, although ascribed to Paul, were certainly not of Pauline origin. These probably come from 90–100 CE or later, and reflect a much more established community than the letters of Paul. Other places where we might look for Jesus and family values are in the letters of James and Peter. If the epistle attributed to James was in fact written by a brother of Jesus, it would probably date before 61 CE; if not, it could be quite late, 70–100 CE. 1 Peter was almost certainly not written by Peter the apostle, and dates from 70–100 CE; 2 Peter followed 1 Peter but was not by the author of 1 Peter. So the epistles range in date from within less than twenty years from the death of Jesus to more than two generations after, and as we shall see, this breadth of time affects the range of attitudes toward family. When we look at Paul's epistles, we include only those which are not disputed, and which may therefore be considered the earliest evidence.

We need to keep two other considerations in mind when we examine these epistles. First, most of them were written to respond to a specific situation or need. The Galatian community, somewhere in Asia Minor (modern Turkey), for example, was being troubled by agitators insisting that pagan converts must undergo circumcision as well as baptism. Whether the situation or need has been imposed from outside the community or something that has arisen from within, it drives the epistle and shapes the advice given. No one can hope to understand any of Paul's letters without taking the context of that or any other letter into account.

Second, we must remember that advice, particularly prohibitive injunctions, usually indicates that the prohibited behavior is happening on a regular basis. As we saw from Matthew, we can read the state of divorce in Jesus' world (and/or Matthew's community) both from his stern prohibition and from the horrified response of the disciples; they think that prohibiting divorce except by reason of adultery renders marriage an untenable proposition. A simple example of this phenomenon in the epistles is Paul's command in 1 Corinthians 14:34 that women should be silent in church. In a world where liturgical roles, whether in Jewish or pagan religion, are usually carefully delineated with regard to gender, the fact that Paul needs to tell women to be silent in community gatherings suggests first, that women feel free to express themselves, and second, that they are doing so with some regularity and a majority of the congregation doesn't have a problem with it. Women in Corinth, in other words, seem to be fully enfranchised in liturgical worship. Were there a significant outcry in the community against it, there would be no need to appeal to Paul, for the community would stop it. This indicates a strong degree of equality between men and women in this community, with the possibility that a similar degree of equality pertains in other early Christian communities. In the case of Corinth, we know that after Paul's visit the worship life has become anarchy; this is the only place where Paul tells the women to keep silent. We also know that individual women figure prominently in community order among Paul's churches, so it is unlikely that this is meant to be a universal prohibition.

A final observation: the word usually translated church, *ekklesia*, appears only three times in the Gospels (Matt. 16:18, 18:17 (twice); in both 18:15 and 18:21 "member of the church" is another NRSV loose translation of "brother," *adelphos*). It appears much more frequently in the epistles, and we need to understand that it does not mean "church" as we understand church today. The word might best be translated "assembly." Such an *ekklesia* was convened in ancient Greek city-states to handle judicial or legislative matters, and it appears in Hellenistic times with similar and broader connotations. The Septuagint, the Greek translation of the Hebrew scriptures, uses it regularly for the Hebrew word *qhl* meaning "assembly"; English translations use "assembly" or "congregation" to translate *qhl* when it appears in Hebrew scriptures. The Greek word appears regularly in first century CE writings, well before there was any general concept of a Christian "church." So when we examine the epistles for community organization, we will find it helpful to remember that the church as we know it does not yet exist, and read "assembly" for "church." Such assemblies of those who believe in Jesus usually met within someone's household, so although the words *oikia* and *oikos* do not drive an examination of family values in the epistles, we should read the texts aware that their communities operate within the context of family. This contrasts in an interesting way with our current perception of the so-called "Christian family" existing within the context of the church and not the other way around. When Paul baptized entire households, these households were incorporated into assemblies of brothers and sisters who met in houses. The early church, therefore, was incubated in the context of families.

Paul and Family Values

While we can extrapolate material about Jesus and family values from the Gospels according to Matthew, Mark, Luke, and John, we cannot find such material in Paul's letters. Paul includes in them nothing of the birth of Jesus, his family, his community, or the details of his life and ministry. If he does know anything about Jesus' life, he has omitted any details. This choice seems deliberate: Paul's entire emphasis is on what the crucifixion and resurrection of Jesus has brought about. Everything else, including Jesus' life before his death, he sets aside. To the Corinthians Paul explains that when he first preached to them, it was not in lofty words or wisdom, but only a crucified Jesus (1 Cor. 2:1–3).

On rare occasions, Paul does refer to traditions about Jesus' death ("from the Lord"), which he received and handed on. For example, in his letter to the Corinthians, Paul recalls a tradition about what Jesus did on the night that he died, but that night itself is of no importance. Nor are any other nights in Jesus' life. What is important, as far as Paul is concerned, is eating and drinking the Lord's body and blood in a worthy manner, waiting for everyone to eat together, and satisfying one's physical hunger at home if it causes one to eat indiscriminately in the community gathering. Similarly, Paul summarizes traditions about Jesus' death and resurrection he has received and which he hands on to the Corinthians, emphasizing the facts of Christ's death, resurrection, and appearances without further details. Christ's death has a salvific purpose. No detailed narrative of Christ's suffering, temptation in Gethsemane, the trial(s), the mocking, or other particulars of the crucifixion occur in Paul.

When Paul does describe Jesus' incarnation in a lovely hymn incorporated into his letter to the Philippians at 2:6–8, it is to portray Jesus as an example of self-giving. The hymn describes a being existing with God who voluntarily self-empties to take human form, and who dies on the cross. No details of Jesus' human birth, life, and ministry are part of this hymn. The hymn has a purpose: Paul uses it here to provide a model of behavior for the Philippian community. As Jesus did not think equality with God a thing to be grasped and hoarded, but freely emptied himself, taking on human existence even to the extent of death on a cross, so members of the Philippian community ought to think of others more highly than themselves and "empty themselves" for others. Paul uses the hymn to exhort the Philippians to behave in ways that model Christ's example, not as a means to explore Christ's human life.

In short, we would be hard put to recreate anything of the Gospels' description of Jesus in the letters of Paul. Indeed, it is fascinating to ask whether any details of Jesus' life and ministry, any of his words or deeds, play any role at all in Pauline letters or theology. Jesus' life is for the most part irrelevant to Paul; his death functions as the means to his resurrection and the salvation of humankind. So it is all the more important to ask how Paul connects the behaviors he commends to communities receiving his letters with the life and death of Jesus. Has Paul in his letters spun advice we could construe as family values from a different cloth than that of the Gospels? Observe first that Paul scarcely uses Jesus' name by itself: instead we find Jesus Christ, Christ Jesus or Lord Jesus. For Paul, Jesus is not "of Nazareth," but Messiah (*Christos* in Greek) and powerful Lord.

Christ's Death Overturns Hierarchy

In fact, it does seem as though Paul's emphasis on the transformative effect of the cross on the way humans see the world and, in particular, on human behavior makes everything else insignificant. For example, to the Philippian and the Corinthian communities, Paul first advocates and then commends community behavior whereby individuals treat each other as esteemed and revered siblings — peers — or as younger sisters or brothers to be cared for as one would a weaker or younger person. To care for a weaker person is to think with the mind of Christ Jesus. As we have seen in the Philippian hymn, this means reflecting and acting on Jesus' refusal to consider equality with God something to be "hoarded," on Jesus' emptying himself, taking a human form, and being born in a human condition as a slave, eventually dying on a cross. With this model in mind, Paul exhorts every member of the Philippian community to consider every other member as better than him or herself and so to follow the example of Christ. Is it any wonder that, in the opening salutation of almost every letter, Paul consistently styles himself a slave of Christ?

Thus we can say that, in distinction to the competitive codes of behavior that secure honor for males, their families, and their households in Roman and Hellenistic culture, the apostle Paul commends to his hearers, first in his visits and then in his letters, notions of community behavior characterized by trust rather than competition, support rather than dominance. Those whom Paul visited and wrote to were among the earliest communities attempting to embody together life in Christ. However, Paul's reason for valuing community members is different from Matthew's. For Matthew, the exclusive authority of the heavenly Father shapes the community as a brotherhood of equal siblings; for Paul, it is Christ's death that inverts ordinary notions of hierarchy.

In other places Paul argues that attributes of Christ like humility and meekness model community behavior. These attributes correlate with the inversion of values that crucifixion represents. As a corollary to thinking of others as better than themselves, Philippians were encouraged to show tolerance and meekness like Christ (4:5). Paul explains how this works when he appeals to the Corinthians "by the meekness and gentleness of Christ" (2 Cor. 10:1). Some at Corinth think Paul's physical presence weak in contrast to the strength of his letters. Paul associates this impression of his weak physical presence with the meekness and gentleness of Christ that is actually strength, not weakness. He makes the argument in the opening chapters of 1 Corinthians that, while the message about crucifixion seems to be a display of weakness, what appears to be foolishness turns out to be in fact the power of God. Paul encourages the Corinthians to contemplate the weakness of the cross, or what seems foolish in the world, rather than their own achievements or abilities. Paul's abilities, like Christ's, are manifest through his weakness not through his accomplishments.

The transformative effect of this way of perceiving the world is a direct result of God's initiative. Paul understands God to use the power of the cross to destroy the wisdom of the wise and to thwart the discernment of the discerning. This is a divine plan foreseen by prophets, as can be seen in Paul's use of Isaiah 29:14 at 1 Corinthians 1:19: "I will destroy the wisdom of the wise. . . . " While members of the Corinthian community seem to have attached importance to the person who baptized each of them, perhaps as a way of valuing some in the community more highly than others, Paul declares that the cross, not baptism, effects a transformed perspective on the world. To see that at the heart of God's love for the universe lies the scandal of the cross, means that all human ways of valuing the world are set aside in favor of a new way of knowing, a way that values what is lowly, scandalous, and despised. This is how Paul understands behavior among community members at Corinth and Philippi to be changed. And it is how Paul's letters have been appropriated and understood in Christian tradition.

In many places Paul valorizes suffering. To the Romans Paul wrote of a life justified by faith in which, having experienced grace, a group of believers may "boast" in their sufferings. Experiencing suffering leads to other qualities, and here Paul describes a chain reaction: suffering effects endurance, endurance produces character, and character leads to hope (Rom. 5:1–5). Paul here interprets sufferings in light of Christ's suffering, particularly his passion and death, and he outlines ways that suffering can have a beneficial effect on individual or corporate character development.

Marriage and Related Matters in Corinth

Neither Augustine nor the Wife of Bath read the NRSV's translation of 1 Corinthians 7:1. Augustine would have been interested, but the Wife of Bath was better at weaving than reading. They were probably both familiar with a Latin translation, however, which translated the verse in the same way as Tyndale, the 1611 Authorized Version, and all the way down to the mid-twentieth-century RSV text: "Now concerning the matters about which you wrote. It is well for a man not to touch a woman." In these translations, Paul is seen to give advice about abstaining from sex. The NRSV proposes instead a sea change: "Now concerning the matters about which you wrote: 'It is well for a man not to touch a woman.'" By enclosing the words "It is well for a man not to touch a woman" in quotation marks, the NRSV committee indicates their belief that these words come from the Corinthians to whom Paul wrote rather than from Paul himself. If it is the Corinthians whom Paul quotes as saying it is good not to have sex with a woman (this is what "touching" here connotes), then it is not Paul but the Corinthians who frame the discussion by rejecting all sexual activity between men and women. Paul may not disagree with them, but it is their words and not his that open the discussion.

If we pause for a moment to try to reconstruct the perspective of those at Corinth who may have coined this statement, we need to recall that at 5:1 Paul describes and condemns a man who is living with his father's wife in the Corinthian community. In the next chapter Paul describes uniting with a prostitute as another kind of sexual behavior at Corinth he condemns. How do these behaviors connect with the Corinthian slogan "It is well for a man not to touch a woman"? Antoinette Clark Wire, in her book *The Corinthian Women Prophets,* proposes a fascinating solution by paying attention to gender. Corinthian men might have been practicing the immorality described in chapters 5 and 6, while Corinthian women might have been promoting the statement "It is good for a person not to touch a woman," especially if some women at Corinth felt led by their devotion to Christ to give up sexual relations. Paul's argument attempts to persuade such women to give up autonomy over their bodies for the well-being of the whole community. He believes that complete abstinence from sexual relations is imprudent and can, in the Corinthian community, lead to the kind of immorality described in 5:1, in which a man is living with his father's wife. For Paul, neither the wife nor the husband are autonomous; both are obligated not to refuse one another sexual relations except for a while in order to devote themselves to prayer after which, Paul concedes, they should come together again.

Paul's prescription of a "time sharing" plan for prayer and for sexual relations may be informed by an apocalyptic tradition familiar to and adopted by the Corinthians describing unusual activities necessitated by living in the last days. The Testament of Naphtali 8:8, for example, speaks about a period before the end wherein there is a time for having intercourse with one's wife and a time to abstain for the purpose of prayer. This would make sense of the apocalyptic flavor of 1 Corinthians 7:29: "Let even those who have wives be as though they had none."

Paul would prefer, however, that all were like him: unmarried, single-minded, and self-controlled in service to God. He advises unmarried people (virgins) and widows to remain single. He advises married people to stay married and not get divorced because this is a charge from the Lord. But if a woman divorces, he proposes that she remain single or be reconciled to her husband. If a man or woman is married to an unbeliever, and the unbelieving partner consents to live together, they should not be divorced since the unbelieving partner is made holy through the other. If the unbelieving partner desires to separate, let them do so. His general principle is to stay as you are, whether circumcised, or single, or married. In the case of slaves, there is some doubt about how to read the general principle. The Greek can be read as urging acceptance of slavery even if there is a chance to gain freedom (NRSV) or it could be read as "If you can gain your freedom be sure to use that opportunity" (RSV). But the two exceptions, slavery and a pagan partner wishing divorce, do not vitiate the principle he gives to the Corinthians of staying in your present condition.

The reason for Paul's advice to the Corinthians to "stay as you are" is due to the impending apocalyptic crisis. Since the "form of this world passing away," the Corinthians need to distance themselves from ordinary human activities. Social institutions like marriage are impermanent and, while Paul does not prohibit men or virgins from marrying, he knows marriage is an occasion for worldly anxieties from which he wishes to spare the Corinthians at a time of apocalyptic crisis.

Some aspects of the Corinthians' situation are unclear and remain so even after two thousand years of interrogation: addressing men, for example, Paul advises that if anyone thinks he is not behaving properly toward his virgin, and if his passions are strong, and it has to be, let him do as he wishes; it is no sin, let them marry. It is fine to marry but it is better, in Paul's judgment, to refrain from marriage. Is Paul here describing an attitude of a Corinthian man to his fiancée (NRSV), or a father responsible for marrying his daughter to someone else? If Paul describes a father and his daughter, the conditional sentence "If his passions are strong" (v. 36) means his anxiety about his daughter remaining unmarried.

We have seen something about Paul's attitudes toward marriage in light of an impending apocalyptic crisis — it is an expedient means to contain passion. What do we know of Paul's attitude toward same-sex relations? To the Roman community (whom he proposes to visit and for whom the letter to the Romans serves as an introduction), Paul describes the dishonorable passions of men for men and women for women as behavior consequent upon idolatry. Here, Paul borrows a well-known theme: the Wisdom of

Solomon 14, for example, describes the immoral sexual behavior of idolatrous people. Because they do not know God, they do not know right or wrong. Sexual perversion, disorder and impurity in marriages, adultery and debauchery are consequences of their error. Yet Romans 1 is not a straightforward discussion of same-sex relations, but of pagan idolatry and its consequences. People have argued that this text is speaking to an ancient reality and not to modern persons, including a minority that holds this text is not about homosexual people, but about heterosexual persons who have exchanged what is natural for what is unnatural.

Of all that could be said about this passage perhaps one thing is necessary. Paul's argument is an old, not a new one. The argument that pagan people in same-sex relations are idolatrous, that is to say, that they do not know God, is an argument that we can debate. Paul may not have known he knew righteous Gentiles in same-sex relations, but we know of examples from the surrounding first-century culture. And we can ask ourselves the same question today: Are there persons in same-sex relationships who worship God? The answer is obvious. Our world, our religious institutions, and our churches are full of same-sex couples seeking to follow Jesus Christ and worship God. Once we can accept that some homosexual people are trying to live holy lives by worshiping God and not idols, then homosexuality cannot itself be a barrier to inclusion within religious communities. This is an argument from experience: if people living in homosexual relationships are attempting to live righteous lives as part of believing communities, homosexual relationships are no longer grounds for exclusion.

A good example of how the primacy of experience is argued over and against tradition within the New Testament is the account in Acts 10 of Peter's vision in Cornelius's house. Luke's account of the baptism of Cornelius and his whole household takes place only after Peter has seen a vision of animals, reptiles, and birds which God invites him to eat. Peter refuses on the grounds that such animals are ritually unclean. Not so, says the voice; "what God has made clean you must not call profane." If animals formerly regarded as unclean are now declared clean by God, Peter now has to rethink who is included as clean within the community. What had once been regarded as unclean is unclean no longer. Peter's speech makes his change of mind and heart clear: "I truly understand that God shows no partiality, but in every nation anyone who fears him and does what is right is acceptable to him." The Holy Spirit falls on all who hear the word, and Peter asks whether anyone can withhold the water for baptizing these people who have received the Holy Spirit. He orders the household of Cornelius baptized forthwith.

Brothers and Sisters

For Paul, God seems to function as *paterfamilias* in local communities. Galatian believers are members of "the household of faith" (Gal. 6:10), and in Romans 12 he describes how to live as followers of Christ, as brothers and sisters.

Paul understands that pride shatters community life. Correcting pride starts with correcting how one thinks about oneself. The brother or sister must not think arrogantly, but with "sober judgment" and self-restraint. The venue for exercising proper self-restraint is the community in which one recognizes different ministries with their different functions. Self-restraint in thought and action allows one to participate fully in and value equally all the various ministries contributing to the unity of the community.

The primary quality of life in Christ is genuine love, that is, love without guile. Here, Paul enumerates community virtues that could be seen as manifestations of the overarching principle of love stemming from God's grace. These are signs of a community's progress in the moral life, that is, life in Christ. The word "progress" reminds us of Luke's summary statements regarding the teenage Jesus' moral and spiritual growth. While Luke is speaking biographically of Jesus, Paul is not so much focused on individual as on community progress: he commends to the community in Rome dispositions or virtues that enhance life together.

Paul recommends above all brotherly love, *philadelphia,* that puts another's interests before one's own. He recommends practical expressions of brotherly love: financial contributions to the needs of the saints and extending hospitality to others. He praises being steadfast in affliction, thinking in harmony toward one another, that is, not thinking oneself intelligent in one's own estimation but associating with the lowly.

Paul's commendation of brotherly love belongs to the language of affiliation by which he consistently addresses fellow believers as "brothers and sisters." In every Pauline letter, the designation identifies new believers as siblings. We have seen in Romans 12 how Paul identifies believers as brothers and sisters, commending to them brotherly love. In Romans 8:29 Paul describes Jesus as "firstborn among many brothers and sisters [NRSV: within a large family]." Using these exhortations Paul creates a new sibling community in which fathers along with their sons and their slaves would now be identified perhaps as "elder brothers" to whom deference and honor is due, or younger brothers who are owed both deference and care. The ordinary use of the words brother and sister to designate community members is emphasized by Paul's exhortation in 1 Corinthians 5:11 not to associate with anyone "called brother" who behaves immorally. One-quarter of the times Paul uses *adelphoi,* however, the NRSV translates it another way — as friend, member of the church, believer, people, beloved, or replaces it with the pronouns their, one, or another. Not only do these misleading translations obscure the constant use of sibling language Paul encourages in new communities, they also sever connections with Paul's image of the newly baptized as adopted sons able to cry, "Abba! Father!" in Galatians 4:5–6 and Romans 8:15.

Paul urges some among the Corinthian recipients of his letters to be humble enough to settle differences not necessarily in one's favor, thus avoiding taking their brothers and sisters to court.

In 1 Corinthians 6:8 he accuses those members of the community who defraud their own siblings. The NRSV's substitution of "believers" for "brothers and sisters" sharply reduces the power of Paul's moral appeal to kinship obligations. Also at 1 Corinthians 8:11, instead of "weak brothers and sisters," the NRSV says, "weak believers for whom Christ died. . . ." In 8:13 Paul declares, "I will never eat meat, so that I may not cause a brother to fall," not the nonspecific translation "one of them" as the NRSV suggests. Paul emphasizes the close responsibility community members have for each other's welfare with his persistent use of sibling language; brothers and sisters have permanent, indissoluble relationships of affection, responsibility, and accountability toward each other.

To be sure, in two places, Paul refers to himself as "father," once as father to the Corinthians and once as one who begot Onesimus, Philemon's slave. I read Philemon as arguing for emancipation of Onesimus although I recognize that Paul's language is unfortunately opaque. It would be helpful to have a clear argument in Paul's letters or in the New Testament for emancipation of slaves, but we don't. Father/son language in Philemon and Corinthians does not so much suggest authority over these individuals or communities as emphasize the deep bond that exists between Paul and the Corinthians and Paul's "begetting" of Onesimus as his child in Christ. True, Paul argues in his letter, Onesimus was Philemon's slave, but, as he was also Paul's brother in Christ, so he is brother to Philemon and should be recognized by Philemon as such. Onesimus will be "owned" when he is received as a brother. Whatever the loss of property involved in the loss of Onesimus as slave, Paul argues, it will be "paid in full" as the recipient receives Onesimus in Christ. Use of the passive verb in the sentence "Perhaps this is the reason *he was separated* from you for a while" (v. 15) suggests that God effected the separation and thus God alone has ownership of Onesimus. Such language moves Onesimus away from relating to Paul as "father" and toward fraternal status as Paul's brother.

While sibling language for new believers characterizes all Pauline writings and Jesus' description of disciples who do the will of God, such language is not unique to the emerging community. In the discussions of associations in chapter 1, we have seen that members of ancient associations before, during, and after the first century identified each other as brothers. It seems likely that Paul's letters and Gospel reports of Jesus' designation as brother, sister, and mother those who do the will of God over and against his biological family are similarly informed by language that we also find in associations of Roman and Hellenistic worlds.

Abraham Malherbe, a specialist in the social scientific context of the New Testament, argues persuasively that the family language suffusing 1 Thessalonians helps new believers replace lost or alienated families of origin. Paul, for example, is like a wet-nurse who breastfeeds new believers. But we should not extend this metaphor too far. In the same letter, Paul is also like a child at the mercy of the Thessalonians' nurture (2:7). Such extraordinary metaphors derive from Paul's image of the cross as power, and wisdom in foolishness.

Paul and Children

A corollary of Paul's advice to "stay as you are" is the absence of any systematic instruction regarding child-rearing in the family. The only "children" Paul cares about are either those adults he brought into life in Christ, or all the brothers and sisters, "we," in relationship to God. This lack of interest in children, and in the life of individual families within the community of believers, results from Paul's conviction that the final coming of Christ is very close; one does not need to be concerned with long-range planning for this world. Paul's ordinary underlying assumptions about children appear in a throw-away line in 2 Corinthians 12:14, where he assures the Corinthians that he will be no burden to them when he visits, because children shouldn't have to provide for parents, but rather parents for their children.

One might object that Paul talks a lot about children, particularly in the NRSV version of Romans and Galatians. In Romans 8:17, as children of God, we are all heirs, and joint heirs with Christ; in Galatians 4:6, because we are children, we cry, "Abba, Father!" The problem lies in the translation. In both Romans and Galatians there are extended passages where although the NRSV refers repeatedly to "children," Paul never had young begotten offspring in mind. The Greek reads *huioi,* sons. Now, unlike *adelphoi,* there is no feminine form of *huioi;* the word for daughters is *thugateres,* and it never appears in these extended passages from Romans and Galatians. However, in 2 Corinthians 6:14–7:1 *thugateres* is used in conjunction with *huioi,* so here we might get a sense of what Paul might have been talking about when he speaks of sons and daughters. This passage includes a string of phrases from the Hebrew scriptures linked together. It reminds the Corinthians that only if they will separate themselves from idolaters and from unclean things (probably food offered in pagan temples) will God be their Father, and they God's sons and daughters. This is the only place in any epistle where *thugateres* is used, but it is useful for pointing out that "sons and daughters" does not imply children, but grown persons with specific responsibilities for their actions.

Similarly, in Romans 8 and 9 and Galatians 4, being sons and calling God "Abba, Father," is not about being the child of a loving daddy. It is about being adopted in order to inherit — in order to be coheirs with Christ of God. "Abba" is a word that would be very foreign to most of these Gentile converts and many Greek-speaking Jews, as one can tell by the fact that it is always accompanied by its Greek equivalent; otherwise it might not be understood. It would be a special word that a full mature member of the community could use as a mark of membership, as a way of claiming that adoption by God and participation in the inheritance.

Despite the NRSV, these passages are not about children. Clearly the NRSV uses the word "children" in these passages to avoid the word "sons." We want Paul to be gender-neutral, but he isn't. In Paul's world Jewish daughters could inherit in the absence of any sons, and Roman daughters could coinherit with sons. Paul mentions women by name managing households and participating in the ministry, and he prescribes behavior for them, so he does not intend to exclude them from the inheritance at all. Perhaps he believes that a mature female believer in Christ becomes a "son," and so an indisputable coinheritor with other sons; this would be fully consistent with there being, in Christ, "no male and female" (Gal. 3:28). But these passages are not about children, but about the entitlement and responsibility of fully adopted heirs of God.

Paul models nurturing behavior toward those whom he guides toward Christ; in 1 Corinthians 4:14 the Greek word for children, *tekna,* is in fact used. But Paul says he has begotten these children through the gospel, and immediately exhorts them to imitate him. So Paul is not interested in perpetuating biological families, and he certainly does not perceive that as being a priority for Jesus, either. The world is coming to an end; there are more important things to do.

Social Order and Family Values after Paul

In the generations after Paul, biblical passages that have come to be called the "household codes" (from *Haustafeln* in Martin Luther's *Shorter Catechism*) describe and prescribe relationships within an estate or household. There are no household codes in Paul's authentic epistles. The household instructions of these later epistles (Col. 3:18–4:1, Eph. 5:22–6:9, 1 Pet. 2:13–3:7, 1 Tim. 2:8–15, and Titus 2:1–10) represent accommodation to traditional hierarchical family structures in the prevailing culture. Most scholars assume a connection between household codes and discussions in antiquity about household management, particularly in Aristotle, Philo, and Josephus. However, these

New Testament epistles lack two features of Paul's letters: both apocalyptic urgency and allusions to specific situations.

Colossians (3:18–4:1) enjoins wives to be subject to their husbands, and children and slaves to obey their parents and earthly masters respectively. Men are addressed in their roles as husbands, fathers, and masters of women, children, and slaves. As husbands they are advised to love their wives and not to treat them harshly. As fathers they are not to provoke their children or they may lose heart. As slave owners they are to treat slaves justly and fairly. Women could have been addressed as *kyria,* the feminine form of *kyrios,* lord, indicating that they were slaveholders. This does not happen in Colossians, although slave owning by the family is assumed, and the omission indicates that the writer of Colossians assumes male preeminence, as does the author's focus on men.

In the preface to the household code, 1 Timothy 2:1–3, the same idea of mutual relationship and responsibility extends to relationships within the wider community. Prayers and intercessions are to be made for everyone, including rulers and those in authority, so that all may lead a peaceable life. Household codes seem to have had varying purposes: perhaps the stress on unity of the Ephesian code illustrates God's intention of unifying all things in Christ. Perhaps the household code in 1 Peter demonstrates the loyalty of Christians to the Roman Empire. In it, believers are instructed to respect government authorities as servants (or slaves) of God. Those addressed as slaves in the household code may be recipients of the letters as well as actual slaves. Thus the entire letter may be written to support acceptance of the status quo in addressing subordinate slaves and women since "the end of all things is near" (4:7). Likewise, the model of Christ is that of a dependent slave: when abused or mistreated he did not retaliate or threaten. When killed, he entrusted himself to God.

The author of Ephesians 5:22–6:9 commands submission of wife to husband as head; subjection of church to Christ as wives to husbands; love of husband to wife; purity of wife; husbands' care and nourishment of their wives as their bodies; obedience of children to parents, obedience of slaves to earthly masters; honor of father and mother; discipline and instruction of children by father; enthusiastic service by slaves; no threatening of slaves by masters.

Christ's offering and sacrifice warrants submission. In 5:21 hearers are enjoined to submit to one another out of reverence for Christ. It seems that the submission of wives receives particular attention: they are told to be subject to their husbands and this injunction is repeated by way of analogy to the subjection of the church to Christ. To submit or be subordinate (*hypotassein*) is a common social concept presupposing recognition of the subordinate as inferior to the superior for the sake of the social good. Paul enjoins the recipients of his letter to the Romans to submit to the law of God (Rom. 8:7 and 10:3) and to civil authority (Rom. 13:1; see also 1 Pet. 2:13). The author of 1 Peter advises younger men to submit to older men (1 Pet. 5:5). As we saw in chapter 2, a teenage Jesus manages to get lost in Jerusalem when his parents and their extended family return to Nazareth without him. Luke, always a preserver of the social order, concludes the event by describing Jesus' return with them and his submission to them (Luke 2:51). Probably to the disciples' astonishment, demons submit to their missionary activity in Luke (10:17, 20). According to Paul, Jesus makes all creation submit to him just as he will transform our humble bodies to the body of his glory (Phil. 3:21). Submission in these cases is by no means a coerced subordination but is done for a higher purpose: to preserve the good of the social order.

The same Christological analogy, made for the submission of wife to husband, is made for the obedience of slaves to masters (Eph. 6:5–9) as if the masters were Christ. Slave owners, that is, masters, also have a master in heaven. Ephesians, while not written by Paul, reflects Paul's theology. Its author has taken motifs about superiority in the notion of headship derived from 1 Corinthians 11:3 and Colossians 1:18 and used them to validate hierarchy: Christ is over man, man over woman, and God over

Christ. Colossians 1:18 adds to Paul's description of the church as the body of Christ by portraying Christ as head of his body, namely, the assembly or local church. But in an extended analogy of Christ as the body, namely, community, Paul in 1 Corinthians 12 animates specific body parts by showing how the head *cannot* say to the feet: I have no need of you. Paul explains that God's arrangement of body parts gives inferior members greater honor. However, Paul's nonhierarchical body in Romans and 1 Corinthians 12 soon disappears. As Carolyn Osiek indicates, with the combination of 1 Corinthians 11:3 and Colossians 1:18, man as head of woman and Christ as head of the church, the stage is set for the combination that occurs in Ephesians: a husband is head of a wife as Christ is head of the church; wife is to body part as husband is to head.

Ephesians also describes marriage in language of ritual washing and purity, whereby the church or bride is presented to her husband without spot or blemish. Here we hear echoes of an old analogy described, for example, in Hosea between unfaithful Israel and God as patient husband. But how exactly does the text argue for the authority of the head over everything else, including the body? It does so through the notion of Christ as savior (5:23). In the Roman world an emperor like Augustus could be a savior figure as a leader who restored peace to the world and protected the weak through military success. Such a leader could be a social leader, i.e., "head."

But how is a wife like a body, specifically the husband's own body? After all, both wives and husbands and other people constitute the believing community. The text simply assumes a male perspective of the impurity and inferiority of women. Only men are addressed in the text: "Each of you should love his wife as himself, and a wife should respect her husband." The assumptions about male and female roles in Ephesians 5 are particular to a time and place in which social order is hierarchically arranged and in which women take on responsibility for subordination. Both analogies and alternatives exist in the surrounding culture.

Harmony in Marriage

Of the values ancient Romans ascribed to a marriage, *concordia,* or harmony between husband and wife, takes pride of place. Marriage is more than a legal state or a monetary transaction; it is a moral bond between individuals. From slaves to senators, in inscriptions and funerary steles, descriptions of male-female relationships as "a partnership in good fortune and in bad" or as "companions" subscribe to this value. The emperor Augustus in 9 CE promulgated his version of "family values" among the upper classes and passed laws prohibiting certain unions on the basis of different status and degree of relation, curtailing divorce and treating adultery as a public crime. Later, Plutarch's *Advice to Bride and Groom* echoes the ethical context of Augustus' laws, regarding as it does the moral development of individuals who marry. Plutarch indicates that the pleasure in marriage needs to be tempered by reason just as married people will need persuasion to attain their mutual desires rather than fighting or quarreling. In his description of "concord," he advises that a man ought to have his household well harmonized who is going to harmonize the city (*polis*), the public forum, and friends. Plutarch's notion of concord, however, includes the duty of the husband to lead his wife to higher morality. Their union is to be a school of orderly behavior in which a hierarchy obtains: the husband teaches the wife qualities of virtue, devotion, constancy, and affection. It is the wife's duty not to trouble or irritate her husband but to live with him in a state of constant meekness, that is, tractability.

In an extended comparison, Plutarch describes the importance of a wife's reception of her husband's seed as a metaphor for sharing with her husband in intellectual advancement. Left to herself she may conceive untoward ideas, low designs and emotions. Plutarch's treatise on upper-class marriage goes beyond Ephesians 5 in its commendation of harmony. While it lacks the analogy of Christ and the church, Plutarch's hierarchical understanding of marriage describes a husband's control over his wife not as an owner has control over a piece of property, but as the soul controls the body, by entering into her feelings and being knit to her through goodwill. Since it is possible to exercise care over the body without being enslaved to its desires, so it is possible to govern a wife and at the same time to make her happy.

My point here is that even though some Christians may look to these later epistles to define relationships between husbands, wives, and children in the contemporary family, we find no commendation of marital virtues like *concordia* in the New Testament. Without recognition of this gap, it is not possible to account for the scarcity of biblical resources encouraging Christian reflection on marriage. However, placing the New Testament in its wider Roman context enables us to grasp that such commendations existed in the first century and that undue emphasis is given to biblical texts like Ephesians 5 simply because there is nothing else in the canon of scripture. Because of the paucity of New Testament resources on the topic, early Christian households conformed to the social ideals and expectations of the surrounding culture.

Conclusion

JESUS AND FAMILY VALUES

THE FLASH POINTS of the current family values debate include the nature of marriage, the roles of family members, and the context in which children should be raised, all topics that presented themselves in quite recognizable and familiar forms to the world of early Christianity. Contraception and abortion, although not explicitly addressed in the New Testament, were practiced in the ancient world. Divorce and second marriages were common. But other topics that lend controversy to the modern discussion of family and family values were completely beyond the possibility of imagination for the early Christian. Unused frozen embryos, in-vitro fertilization, and stem cell research would have been far more incomprehensible to the ancient mind than deity-assisted virginal or post-menopausal conception appear to us. Gay couples living together openly, with biological or adopted children and some societal protections, would have been equally incomprehensible. Contemporary notions of individual privacy and separation of church and state would have boggled the first-century mind, while many of today's major Christian denominations have excised from their lectionaries New Testament passages that prescribe the treatment of slaves and silence women in church.

The Canaanite woman induced Jesus to revise his own operating principles in the light of new experience and understanding.

This story provides a prime example for the use of scripture in life. First, it is a story about redrawing the boundaries of inclusion. When it opens, Jesus has withdrawn outside the boundaries of Israel to the coastal regions of Tyre and Sidon. But he has not withdrawn beyond public notice. An anonymous woman cries out to Jesus in language he understands, "Have mercy on me, O Lord, Son of David; my daughter is severely possessed by a demon." He makes no response. Then the disciples ask him to send her away, and he tells her why: "I was sent only to the lost sheep of the house of Israel." Faced with her second plea for help, Jesus explains that his mission to Israel is not to be snatched away and thrown to the dogs. Only when the woman retorts that even the dogs eat crumbs that fall from their masters' table does Jesus publicly acknowledge her faith. Her daughter is healed instantly. The organizational challenges faced by early Jewish Christian communities devolved upon setting and maintaining boundaries, and that is reflected in the New Testament documents. But the story of the Canaanite woman shows us something else. Matthew didn't go back through the manuscript and scrape out all the places where Jesus said he was sent only to the lost sheep of the house of Israel, but instead showed how Jesus, the ultimate paradigm for the believing community, revisited and revised an assessment of who gets included in the kingdom.

In Acts 10, Luke does the same thing with Peter, describing a vision where God reveals to Peter that the Torah requirements for ritual purity no longer operate as barriers to inclusion in the community of those who accept Jesus. Peter, walking out on deep water, receives the revelation, reports it, and acts on it; but the community finds its implications unbearable, and subsequently imposes its own small set of barriers, far less onerous but barriers nonetheless. Gentiles should abstain from the pollutions of idols, from unchastity, from what has been strangled, and from blood (Acts 15:19–20). Even so, the inclusiveness of the early Christian community was one of the factors that contributed to the bad reputation it had with political authorities.

Just as we seek guidance in scriptures that are thousands of years removed from us, the actors and authors in those writings also sought guidance in their scriptures and showed us how. Paul is a prime example of this; he honors the scripture by wrestling with it, and while some of his interpretative maneuvers are opaque to us, his intention to be responsible to scripture shines through clearly. We cannot responsibly excise bits of scripture or deny what they meant in their own context, insofar as the meaning is accessible to us. But we can study the patterns of scripture, the direction of scripture, the underlying major themes in scripture, and bring those to bear on the interpretation of those passages which seem confined to the time and place when they were first written.

Paul's letters, among the oldest parts of the New Testament, commend "staying as you are" in light of impending apocalyptic catastrophe. For this reason, Paul counsels the Corinthian community in single-minded devotion to the Lord over and above the exercise of passion for which marriage is the containment. To community members whom he calls "brothers (and sisters)" Paul commends humility, patient affection, and competition in honoring each person in the body of Christ, that is, "sober judgment." After Paul, the authors of the "household codes" counsel wives, children, and slaves to obey their husbands, fathers, and masters. The author of Ephesians borrows the analogy of Christ and the church, enjoining husbands to cherish wives as they would their own bodies, while wives submit to husbands as the church submits to Christ.

Jesus, like Paul, identifies disciples or community members as siblings in a family focused on doing the will of the one heavenly Father. In Mark, Jesus prohibits divorce unequivocally, but in Matthew's Gospel Jesus allows divorce under a single circumstance — adultery. In Matthew, certain disciples make themselves "eunuchs for the sake of the kingdom" as unmarried examples of single-minded devotion to God, an idea that is absent from the other Gospels. Married disciples in Matthew, Mark, and Luke profess to have left wives, families, professions, and households to follow Jesus. In some passages, Jesus commands his would-be followers to repudiate family, wealth, and property for the sake of the kingdom; in others, he commands individuals to return to family and community.

Thus the New Testament portrays a variety of ways in which the early believers became followers of Jesus in the differing circumstances of single, married, and community life. For us to isolate and commend one set of moral instructions over another fails to acknowledge the authority of the whole teaching. There is no unified teaching on marriage, divorce, households, or families in the New Testament. Since we can find implicit commendations of differing patterns of life — or, if you will, New Testament "lifestyles" — in various communities, it would seem imprudent to single out any one form of behavior as authoritative. All must be regarded as provisional, since other models might rightfully also derive their authority from the New Testament. Furthermore, a multiplicity of community and personal life patterns is explicitly warranted by Paul's celebration of the diversity that constitutes the body of Christ. Similarly, the authority of the Gospel is self-limiting and self-defining through the very fact that the church has canonized four distinct, often irreconcilably different, and equally authoritative Gospel witnesses.

It is very important to pay attention to the sociological and literary contexts of the Gospels and Paul's letters. To understand Jesus' own household, the so-called "Holy Family" of Matthew's Gospel or the extended family of Luke, or the households from which disciples come, we need to take the contours of Roman households into account: husbands, wives, children, extended family members, slaves, and adopted children could and did characterize middle-sized households in outlying places of the empire, including Galilee. Family members also belonged to guilds in which members called each other "brothers." Literary context, on the other hand, shapes meaning and helps to interpret passages in light of a whole text. When we hear readings from the

Old Testament, the epistles, or the Gospels, we are encountering only isolated fragments of a larger whole. It is important to know that the version of the Lord's Prayer closest to the one we say in worship today occurs in the heart of the Sermon on the Mount, the first extended teaching of Jesus in Matthew's Gospel. Jesus teaches the disciples (and others who may have heard the sermon) a concise prayer, the praying of which brings the community of the heavenly Father into being. Similarly, today we say the Lord's Prayer together in the Eucharist just at the point before we receive communion. As part of the community of the heavenly Father we say the Lord's Prayer together, petitioning God for the bread that sustains our lives.

We may also visualize a literary description through art. An icon or painting called *The Holy Family in Egypt,* depicting Joseph, Mary, and the infant Jesus in Mary's arms, may look like any husband, wife, and child. I know it is Matthew because they are in Egypt, and so I can "read" this picture as a representation of Matthew's description of Joseph taking "the child and his mother" into and out of Egypt. In Matthew, Joseph is not the father of the child. The family may be holy, but it is not a husband, wife, and their child. Christian tradition has understood Matthew's wording to imply a distance between Joseph on the one hand and "the child and his mother" on the other. Thus, even if Joseph, Mary, and her child look like a family unit, deeper investigation reveals that a closer analogy to the Holy Family may be to a family in which the child is born of the mother with an adoptive father.

By contrast, depictions of the Holy Family in Luke do not locate the "family" in Egypt but portray the infant Jesus with an older child, John, and his mother, Elizabeth. Luke's accounts of the births of John the Baptist and Jesus focus on the relationship of the cousins, Elizabeth and Mary, and their miraculous births; they include characters like Elizabeth and Zechariah, Anna and Simeon, who appear nowhere else in the New Testament. Luke's notion of an extended family is of a piece with his larger vocabulary for houses and households, including terms for inns and innkeepers, the verb "to receive as a guest," and descriptions of a household that would terrify most of us: father, mother, son, daughter, and daughter's mother-in-law. Luke describes large houses with domestic and outdoor servants, medium houses with a few slaves, and poorer houses without slaves of any kind.

Reading ancient texts like the Gospels or letters of Paul is hard work. It's not just a question of investigating ancient sociological or literary contexts; it's a question of asking critical questions about bringing ancient texts to bear on modern realities. Our interrogation of ancient texts, more often than not, lays bare not so much the texts as our own presuppositions. But our fidelity to these texts and their authority for us makes it imperative that we continue to do it in full awareness of the provisional character of our readings and applications.

What does this look like in practice for twenty-first-century Christians? If it looks like irreconcilably different worshippers gathered around the table of the Last Supper and celebrating salvation by Jesus Christ in vastly divergent patterns of life, is that not entirely congruent with the multiple witnesses presented in scripture? Can we consciously and as a matter of policy exclude any member of the body of Christ without damaging the whole? When I kneel side by side with someone whose construction of family looks radically different from mine, I witness to a God whose ways are not our ways, whose judgments cannot be limited by our finite understanding, whose generosity and creativity must not be circumscribed by our tiny hearts and minds.

Our decision to include all forms of family in the community of God may be misguided. Some configurations of family may be tares in the wheat of God's kingdom. But, as Gamaliel said in Acts 5:38–39, "if this plan or this undertaking is of human origin, it will fail; but if it is of God, you will not be able to overthrow them." If we condemn, we contravene God's own commandments. The sure knowledge we have is that if we err on the side of generosity and magnanimity, we do not stray far from the nature of God, and we have a sure claim on God's forgiveness.

An old rabbi once asked his pupils how they could tell when the night had ended and the day had begun. "Could it be," asked one student, "when you can see an animal in the distance and tell whether it's a sheep or a dog?" "No," answered the rabbi. Another asked, "Is it when you can look at a tree in the distance and tell whether it's a fig tree or a peach tree?" "No," answered the rabbi. "Then when is it?" the pupils demanded. "It is when you can look on the face of any person and see that it is your sister or brother. Because if you cannot see this, it is still night."

My parents' fiftieth wedding anniversary included married, single, divorced, and remarried relatives alongside people like me in a same-sex, committed relationship. As they have suffered their relatives' deaths and divorces, and celebrated marriages and remarriages, births and blendings of families, my parents have tried to maintain relationships with all present and past family members. They have attended second marriages other relatives shunned. They visit and are visited by ex-wives and ex-husbands of their relatives with their children. Were these persons to marry again, I know my parents would welcome the newly constituted families into their home.

So it was at my parents' fiftieth wedding anniversary, listening to my mother's talk at a church service planned by my father, I sat with my same-sex partner next to my intentionally single brother. Afterward I enjoyed lunch in the company of my mother's cousin and his second ex-wife. No one who knows my parents thinks that everyone in their family shares their perspectives, or that their generosity was not hard-won. They would be the first to admit its imperfections. But its simplicity is utterly genuine and grounded in reliance upon God's limitless love. On such occasions, "surrounded by so great a crowd of witnesses," focusing on thanking God for the blessings of a marriage enables the joys and sorrows of family presence and absence to be subordinate to gratitude. These are the circumstances that make such celebrations richer by far and give us a strange and poignant foretaste of the messianic banquet. This is the place where the day has begun.

Appendix

Easy Reference Chart

This easy reference chart shows the variety of Greek house language used in the Gospels along with the New Revised Standard Version. The chart includes all Greek words derived from the words for house and household, *oikia* and *oikos,* including nouns, verbs, verbs used as nouns (participles), adjectives, and adverbs. The chart does not include places where the NRSV uses "house," "home," or "family" to render Greek terms apart from *oikia* and *oikos* even if these terms indicate a household context, such as "member of the family" for *adelphos,* "brother." We can see from the chart that *oikos* and *oikia* dominate, with *oikeo* in compound participle forms such as "one who dwells" in third place.

The chart is offered as an entry point into an examination of house language in the New Testament, which will lead readers into their own insights and interpretations. Among the Gospels, Luke uses house language most and John least. Matthew uses the term *oikodespotes,* master of the house, landowner, more than anyone else, perhaps reflecting interest in community as household.

John, on the other hand, reflecting a community under siege, is not interested in earthly households. Where Luke would "make a home" somewhere, John uses the verb *meno,* remain or stay, connoting impermanence. The NRSV injects house language into John at least six times, obscuring John's sense of earthly transience. "My Father's house" is the one that matters in John.

A similar phenomenon occurs when the NRSV uses "home" and "family," terms that we connect with domestic stability, to represent house and household. In Matthew's Gospel, Joseph, the child, and his mother "make their home" in Nazareth; and Jesus leaves Nazareth and "makes his home" in Capernaum, translated *katoikeo*, "inhabit" or "reside."

In Mark's Gospel (2:1), Jesus is "at home" in his house in Capernaum. Frequent use of *oikos/oikia* for ordinary houses in the first part of Mark contrasts with its use for the Temple in Jerusalem ("house of God") at the end of Jesus' journey. Perhaps Mark's community was a collection of house groups in the Decapolis of Galilee.

You can see from this chart that the words *oikos* and *oikia*, as well as appearing in their own right, are also compounded with other lexical components to create expanded meanings from the root *oikos/oikia*. Places where *oikeo-* compounds are referred to indicate that the sense of the verb *oikeo* is extended by some other word. Where the compounds are too complicated to render into English, they are referred to simply as an *oikeo-* compound. The phrase *oikeo-* compound does not reflect a single origin but rather a list of compound verbs including *katoikeo, perioikeo,* and *paroikeo.*

The creating of nouns and adjectives from verbs, i.e., the use of participles, is a far more significant element of Greek than English. For the sake of clarity, when a word appears in English as a noun or adjective but actually reflects a Greek verb participle, the chart identifies it as a participle.

MATTHEW

English NRSV word	Greek word	Text Ref
builder	oikodomeo participle	Matt. 21:42
building	oikodome	Matt. 24:1
deportation	metoikesia	Matt. 1:11
		Matt. 1:12
		Matt. 1:17(x2)
home	oikia	Matt. 8:6
		Matt. 17:25
	oikos	Matt. 9:6
		Matt. 9:7
house	oikia	Matt. 2:11
		Matt. 5:15
		Matt. 7:24
		Matt. 7:25
		Matt. 7:26
		Matt. 7:27
		Matt. 8:14
		Matt. 9:10
		Matt. 9:23
		Matt. 9:28
		Matt. 10:12
		Matt. 10:13
		Matt. 10:14
		Matt. 12:25
		Matt. 12:29
		Matt. 13:1
		Matt. 13:36
		Matt. 13:57
		Matt. 19:29
		Matt. 24:17
		Matt. 24:43
		Matt. 26:6
	oikos	Matt. 12:4
		Matt. 12:44
		Matt. 21:13(x2)
		Matt. 23:38
house of (family line)	oikos	Matt. 10:6
		Matt. 15:24
household	oiketeia (variant: oikia)	Matt. 24:45
householder	oikodespotes	Matt. 13:27

MATTHEW

English NRSV word	Greek word	Text Ref
landowner	oikodespotes	Matt. 20:1
		Matt. 20:11
		Matt. 21:33
master of the house	oikodespotes	Matt. 13:52
		Matt. 24:43
members of a household	oikiakos	Matt. 10:36
one who dwells	oikeo- compound participle	Matt. 23:21
palace	oikos	Matt. 11:8
those of a household	oikiakos	Matt. 10:25
to build	oikodomeo	Matt. 7:24
		Matt. 7:26
		Matt. 16:18
		Matt. 21:33
		Matt. 23:29
		Matt. 26:61
	oikodomeo participle	Matt. 27:40
to live with	oikeo- compound	Matt. 12:45
to make home	oikeo- compound	Matt. 2:23
		Matt. 4:13
world	oikoumene	Matt. 24:14

MARK

English NRSV word	Greek word	Text Ref
builder	oikodomeo participle	Mark 12:10
building	oikodome	Mark 13:1
		Mark 13:2
home	oikia	Mark 13:34
	oikos	Mark 2:1
		Mark 2:11
		Mark 3:19
		Mark 5:19
		Mark 7:30
		Mark 8:3
		Mark 8:26

MARK

English NRSV word	Greek word	Text Ref
house	oikia	Mark 1:29
		Mark 2:15
		Mark 3:25
		Mark 3:27
		Mark 6:4
		Mark 6:10
		Mark 7:24
		Mark 9:33
		Mark 10:10
		Mark 10:29
		Mark 10:30
		Mark 12:40
		Mark 13:15
		Mark 13:35
		Mark 14:3
	oikos	Mark 2:26
		Mark 5:38
		Mark 7:17
		Mark 9:28
		Mark 11:17
lived	katoikesis	Mark 5:3
owner of the house	oikodespotes	Mark 14:14
to build	oikodomeo	Mark 14:58
	oikodomeo participle	Mark 15:29

LUKE

English NRSV word	Greek word	Text Ref
builder	oikodomeo participle	Luke 20:17
home	oikos	Luke 1:23
		Luke 1:56
		Luke 5:24
		Luke 5:25
		Luke 8:39
		Luke 9:61
		Luke 15:6
		Luke 16:4
		Luke 18:14

LUKE

English NRSV word	Greek word	Text Ref
house	oikia	Luke 4:38
		Luke 5:29
		Luke 6:48
		Luke 6:49
		Luke 7:6
		Luke 7:37
		Luke 7:44
		Luke 8:27
		Luke 8:51
		Luke 9:4
		Luke 10:5
		Luke 10:7
		Luke 15:8
		Luke 15:25
		Luke 17:31
		Luke 18:29
		Luke 20:47
		Luke 22:10
		Luke 22:11
		Luke 22:54
	oikos	Luke 1:40
		Luke 6:4
		Luke 7:10
		Luke 7:36
		Luke 8:41
		Luke 11:17
		Luke 11:24
		Luke 12:39
		Luke 13:35
		Luke 14:1
		Luke 14:23
		Luke 16:27
		Luke 19:5
		Luke 19:9
		Luke 19:46
house of (family line)	oikos	Luke 1:27
		Luke 1:33
		Luke 1:69
		Luke 2:4
household	oikos	Luke 12:52
live	oikeo- compound	Luke 11:26
management	oikonomia	Luke 16:2

LUKE

English NRSV word	Greek word	Text Ref
manager	oikonomia	Luke 16:4
	oikonomos	Luke 12:42
		Luke 16:1
		Luke 16:3
		Luke 16:8
neighbor	oikeo- compound participle	Luke 1:65
	oikos- compound	Luke 1:58
one who built	oikodomeo participle	Luke 6:48
		Luke 6:49
one who lives	oikeo- compound participle	Luke 13:4
owner of the house	oikodespotes	Luke 12:39
		Luke 13:25
		Luke 14:21
sanctuary	oikos	Luke 11:51
slave	oiketes	Luke 16:13
stranger	oikeo- compound	Luke 24:18
to be built	oikodomeo	Luke 6:48
to build	oikodomeo	Luke 11:47
		Luke 11:48
		Luke 12:18
		Luke 14:28
		Luke 14:30
world	oikoumene	Luke 2:1
		Luke 4:5
		Luke 21:26

JOHN

English NRSV word	Greek word	Text Ref
home	oikos	John 7:53
		John 11:20
house	oikia	John 11:31
		John 12:3
		John 14:2
	oikos	John 2:16
		John 2:17
household	oikia	John 4:53
		John 8:35
under construction	oikodomeo	John 2:20

SELECTED BIBLIOGRAPHY

Barclay, John M. G. "The Family as the Bearer of Religion in Judaism and Early Christianity." In *Constructing Early Christian Families: Family as Social Reality and Metaphor,* ed. Halvor Moxnes. New York: Routledge, 1997

Barr, James. "Abba Isn't Daddy." *Journal of Theological Studies* 39, no. 1 (1988): 28–47.

Bartchy, Scott S. "Undermining Ancient Patriarchy: The Apostle Paul's Vision of a Society of Siblings." *Biblical Theology Bulletin* 29, no. 2 (Summer 1999): 68–78.

Bauckham, Richard J. "All in the Family: Identifying Jesus' Relatives." *Biblical Archaeology Society* (April 2000).

Cloke, Gillian. "Mater or Martyr: Christianity and the Alienation of Women within the Family in the Later Roman Empire." *Theology and Sexuality* 5 (1996): 37–57.

Coloe, Mary. Review of *House Church and Mission: The Importance of Household Structures in Early Christianity,* by Roger W. Gehring. *Review of Biblical Literature* (February 2005).

Cox, Cheryl Anne. *Household Interests: Property, Marriage Strategies, and Family Dynamics in Ancient Athens.* Princeton, NJ: Princeton University Press, 1998.

Destro, Adriana, and Pesce Mauro. "Fathers and Householders in the Jesus Movement: The Perspective of the Gospel of Luke." *Biblical Interpretation* 11, no. 2 (2003): 211–38.

Elliott, John H. "The Jesus Movement Was Not Egalitarian but Family-Oriented." *Biblical Interpretation* 9, no. 1 (2003): 173–210.

George, Michele. "Domestic Architecture and Household Relations: Pompeii and Roman Ephesos." *Journal for the Study of the New Testament* 27, no. 1 (September 2004): 7–25.

Harland, Philip A. "Familial Dimensions of Group Identity: 'Brothers' in Associations of the Greek East." *Journal of Biblical Literature* 124, no. 3 (2005): 491–513.

Hezser, Catherine. "The Impact of Household Slaves on the Jewish Family in Roman Palestine." *Journal for the Study of Judaism* 34, no. 4 (2003): 375–424.

Johnson, Elizabeth E. "Apocalyptic Family Values." *Interpretation* 56, no. 1 (January 2002): 34–44.

Köstenberger, Andreas. *God, Marriage, and Family: Rebuilding the Biblical Foundation.* Wheaton, IL: Crossway Books, 2004.

Lawler, Michael G., and Gail S. Risch. "Covenant Generativity: Toward a Theology of Christian Family." *Horizons* 26, no. 1 (Spring 1999): 7–30.

MacDonald, Margaret. "Domestic Space and Families in Early Christianity: Editor's Introduction." *Journal for the Study of the New Testament* 27, no. 1 (September 2004): 3–6.

MacIntyre, Alasdair. "Fully Alive, Informed by Virtue." Review of *The Good Life: Ethics and the Pursuit of Happiness,* by Herbert McCabe. *The Tablet,* September 10, 2005: 22.

Madigan, Kevin. "Ancient and High-Medieval Interpretations of Jesus in Gethsemane: Some Reflections on Tradition and Continuity in Christian Thought." *Harvard Theological Review* 88, no. 1 (1995): 157–73.

Miller, Johnathan. "March of the Conservatives: Penguin Film as Political Fodder." *New York Times,* September 13, 2005, September 17, 2005, www.nytimes.com.

Mollenkott, Virginia Ramey. "Diverse Forms of Family Mentioned or Implied in the Hebrew and Christian Scriptures." *Sensuous Spirituality: Out from Fundamentalism.* New York: Crossroad, 1992, 194–97.

"Moral Impurity and the Temple in Early Christianity in Light of Ancient Greek Practice and Qumranic Ideology." *Harvard Theological Review* 97, no. 4 (2004): 383–411.

Moxnes, Halvor. "Seeing with Families." *Biblical Interpretation* 11, no. 2 (2003): 115–18.

Norman, Naomi J. "Death and Burial of Roman Children: The Case of the Yasmina Cemetery at Carthage — Part I, Setting the Stage." *Mortality* 7, no. 3 (2002): 302–23.

Osiek, Carolyn. "The Family in Early Christianity: 'Family Values' Revisited." *Catholic Biblical Quarterly* 58 (1996): 1–25.

———. "Marriage and Family in the Biblical World." *Catholic Biblical Quarterly* 67, no. 2 (April 2005): 378–79.

———. "*Pietas* In and Out of the Frying Pan." *Biblical Interpretation* 9, no. 1 (2003): 166–72.

Osiek, Carolyn, and Margaret Y. MacDonald. *A Woman's Place: House Churches in Earliest Christianity.* Minneapolis: Fortress, 2006.

Painter, John. "When Is a House Not Home? Disciples and Family in Mark 3:13–35." *New Testament Studies* 45, no. 4 (1999): 498–513.

Penn, Michael. "Performing Family: Ritual Kissing and the Construction of Early Christian Kinship." *Journal of Early Christian Studies* 10 (1999): 105–38.

Rawson, Beryl. "'The Roman Family' in Recent Research: State of the Question." *Biblical Interpretation* 11, no. 2 (2003): 119–38.

Regev, Eyal. "Moral Impurity and the Temple in Early Christianity in Light of Ancient Greek Practice and Qumranic Ideology." *Harvard Theological Review* 97, no. 4 (2004): 383–411.

Richardson, Peter. "Towards a Typology of Levantine/Palestinian Houses." *Journal for the Study of the New Testament* 27, no. 1 (2004): 47–68.

Scheidel, W. "Brother-Sister Marriage in Roman Egypt." *Journal of Biosocial Science* 29 (1997): 361–71.

Schneiders, Sandra M. "'Because of the Woman's Testimony . . .': Reexamining the Issue of Authorship in the Fourth Gospel." *New Testament Studies* 44 (1998): 513–35.

Seim, Turid Karlsen. "Descent and Divine Paternity in the Gospel of John: Does the Mother Matter?" *New Testament Studies* 51, no. 3 (2005): 361–75.

Standhartinger, Angela. "The Origin and Intention of the Household Code in the Letter to the Colossians." *Journal for the Study of the New Testament* 79, no. 1 (September 2000): 117–30.

Steinfels, Peter. "A Church That Can and Cannot Change: Dogma." *New York Times*, May 22, 2005, www.nytimes.com.

Stout, Harry S. "Word and Order in Colonial New England." *The Bible in America: Essays in Cultural History*, ed. Nathan O. Hatch and Mark A. Noll. New York: Oxford University Press, 1982.

Tyson, Joseph B. "Guess Who's Coming to Dinner: Peter and Cornelius in Acts 10:1–11:18." *Forum New Series* 2, no. 2 (Fall 1999): 179–95.

Van Der Watt, J. G. "Ethics in First John: A Literary and Socioscientific Perspective." *Catholic Biblical Quarterly* 61, no. 4 (1999): 491–511.

Wilgoren, Jodi. "'Mothering the Mother' during Childbirth, and After." *New York Times*, September 25, 2005.

Winter, Sara C. "Paul's Letter to Philemon." *New Testament Studies* 33, no. 3 (1987): 1–15.